Safe to Drink?

The Quality of

Your Water

Safe to Drink?

The Quality of
Your Water

by Julie Stauffer

New Futures 9

CENTRE FOR
ALTERNATIVE
TECHNOLOGY
PUBLICATIONS

© August 1996
The Centre for Alternative Technology Machynlleth, Powys, SY20 9AZ, UK
Tel. 01654 702400 • **Fax**. 01654 702782
Email: cat@gn.apc.org • **Web page:** http://www.foe.co.uk/CAT

Written by Julie Stauffer
Assistance Peter Harper, Graham Preston, Linda Thomas, Lesley Bradnam,
James Saper, Clive Newman, Chris Weedon, Rick Dance
Illustrations Graham Preston and Maritsa Kelly
Cover Photos Main: Science Photo Library; Background: Albatross Editions
Assistant Editor Jules Lesniewski
Editor and Designer Dave Thorpe

ISBN 1 898049 19 X
First Edition August 1996.

Mail Order copies from: Buy Green By Mail.   Tel. 01654 703409
Trade Distribution: Biblios, Star Road, W. Sussex, RH13 8LD.   Tel. 01403 710 971

Published with the invaluable assistance of Environment Wales,
a branch of the Welsh Office.

The author

Julie Stauffer was born and raised in Toronto, Canada. She studied biology and journalism in Ontario and now is a freelance writer and editor specialising in health, science and environmental issues. She has spent the last few years researching and writing about water and sewage Her work includes *The Big Flush* - an educational video on sewage issues. *Safe to Drink?* was written whilst Julie was a volunteer at the Centre for Alternative Technology. Since returning to Canada she has begun work on a book concerned with water pollution. Her interests, when not examining her tap water, include hiking, cycling and canoeing.

Contents

Foreword

The provision of good, clean water has been the single greatest achievement of public health in the last two centuries. From Edwin Chadwick's *Report on the Sanitary Conditions of the Labouring Population of Great Britain* in 1842, to the death of Prince Albert from typhoid in 1861, there was a revolution in understanding the importance of clean water in preventing the spread of such killer diseases as cholera and typhoid. This led the reforming Victorians to undertake the great public water works which still form the basis of our water services today.

In contrast, the period also saw the final stages of the decimation of the British rural economy and the rise of the mono-culture agriculture, resulting from the Enclosures Acts. The contrast is revealing, for in the first case we had the public-sector funding of the provision of drinkable water for the vast majority of the population, a provision not available for much of this century. The same cannot be said for the private provision of food from privately owned land. Britain leads the world for having some of the highest rates of dietary disease and nutritionally poorly balanced diets, and much of the resulting unnecessary suffering and death can be attributed to intensive farming and the highly concentrated food industry, and the products they promote.

We now live in an era when the water services themselves are being 'enclosed' and taken from public to private or at least share-holder, ownership. It raises the questions over the willingness of commercial market-driven companies to provide the best public benefits, and the ability of public regulators to ensure that they do. The public are suspicious and increasingly turn to alternative sources of water and water-based products rather than drink water from the tap.

This isn't just a fussy fad for a few better-off, water-filter purists. A 1994 survey of children under five found that a majority no longer drink water. They drink, of course, but their parents prefer to give them soft drinks or bottled water - in part from a fear that tap water is not good enough. They are not convinced that a private company will put children's health ahead of profits.

This book does not provide all the answers, but it does provide some of them, and the essential tools needed to get the rest. It helps us ask the right questions about the quality of water and about the activities of companies that supply water, so that we can evaluate the answers we get. We may not see a publicly-owned water system in Britain again, but we can expect a publicly accountable regulator to ensure that the industry acts in the public's best interests. Using this book, we can watch the industry, and watch the regulator who watches the industry and if necessary, we can take action to get the changes we want.

Tim Lobstein
Co-director
The Food Commission

Chapter 1
Life-Blood

Drinking water concerns us all. We need clean water to live, and we need adequate supplies of it. Lately, however, the quality and quantity of drinking water in the UK has received a lot of bad press: water shortages, cryptosporidiosis outbreaks, accidental chemical leaks and spills.

Privatisation of the water industry in England and Wales has generated controversy and criticism. More and more people are losing faith in the quality of their tap water and are turning to home filtering systems or bottled water.

However, is this pessimism about our water supply really justified? On one hand, the answer is yes. There are problems with supply and over-abstraction. Costs to consumers have risen exorbitantly. Thousands of chemicals are finding their way into our water supplies every year. Some cause cancer, some disrupt hormone systems, some are toxic in very small quantities. And because many of these chemicals don't break down quickly, they build up in the water cycle. If nothing is done, the situation will continue to get worse.

Nonetheless, there are also reasons for optimism. Modern treatment systems ensure that the water in our taps, generally speaking, is clean, reliable and plentiful. Water-borne epidemics no longer claim thousands of lives — you're not going to get cholera or typhoid fever from your drinking water.

While there is concern about being exposed to small quantities of chemicals that may cause cancer if you ingest them over long periods of time, at the moment the risk is minimal. Overall, the quality of our tap water is very good.

Most importantly, the means to make our water cleaner are simple and readily available. If we stop putting chemicals into our water supply, they won't turn up in our tap. What we need are stricter regulations on industrial effluent, pesticide use, and municipal sewage, and better safeguards against leaks and spills of dangerous chemicals.

This book gives you the facts about your drinking water. It describes how water gets from its source to your tap. It explains how drinking water can become contaminated, what the most common contaminants are, and which ones are worth worrying about. It looks at the management and regulation of the water industry. Also it focuses on the potentially increasing problems posed by droughts to both the individual consumer and the suppliers of water It tells you what to do if you're not happy with your supply. It weighs the pros and cons of bottled water and filtered water.

Finally, it outlines the process of obtaining, storing and treating an independent water supply if you're not on the mains. You'll find a glossary of technical terms at the back of the book, and a resource guide that lists relevant organisations, suppliers and consultants.

What is water?

Water — simply the conjunction of two hydrogen atoms with an oxygen atom — is an amazingly versatile, surprising and powerful substance.

Life on earth would be impossible without it. It forms 70% of the mass of the human body, for example. It conducts electricity, and this property allows it to become the medium for communication between cells in living organisms — as well as giving you an electric shock if you happen to drop the radio into the bath while you're in it!

It is a vehicle for communication in another way too: it can carry heat energy and solutions, molecules or ions of many other substances, such as salts, gases and minerals. These may then

How much water is there?

Accessible fresh water is only a tiny fraction of the total global water resources.

---

travel with it into places they would otherwise never reach, which has all sorts of implications for soil leaching, for the availability of nutrients to plants and animals, and for pollution.

Scientists are still discovering new things about this apparently most familiar of substances. Some recent research, for example, suggests that water may have a 'memory', which allows it to carry an electromagnetic imprint of substances it has recently been in contact with — the basis of homœopathic remedies — which could in future reveal further fundamental relationships between the subtle condition of water, our health and the environment.

Water exists in many forms: not just ice, water and steam, but different types of each, which behave differently under different conditions. Each form has different structural properties: the fluid form itself can be immensely strong, allowing it to move rocks and crack them as it freezes and thaws. Plants exploit this strength to support themselves and we exploit it in hydraulic mechanics. The energy in the gaseous form is used in steam turbines. When it becomes solid it expands; this phenomena causes erosion in rocks and buildings.

The ability of water to change form gives rise to the water cycle of precipitation, evaporation and condensation, a fundamental component of global and local weather systems.

Only a fixed amount of water is drinkable; and we keep recycling it over and over. New water is not being created at a

The Hydrological Cycle

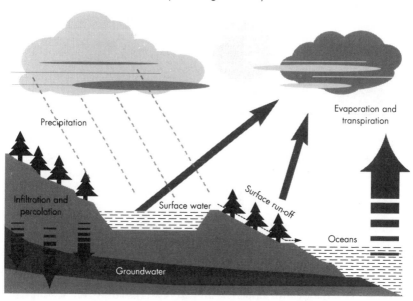

Precipitation

Evaporation and transpiration

Infiltration and percolation

Surface water

Surface run-off

Oceans

Groundwater

Water constantly cycles between clouds, surface water, underground aquifers, and oceans. This hydrological cycle is driven by the energy of sun.

significant rate, nor is existing water destroyed for ever. For this reason it is quite likely that at some point in your life you may have drunk molecules of what was once Francis Drake's bathwater and bathed in molecules of what was once Jane Austin's urine.

It is fortunate for us that many naturally occurring processes constantly clean this water. These are the subject of a companion volume, *Sewage Solutions: Answering the Call of Nature*. For now, let us look at where water comes from in more detail.

Where does it come from?

Water seems like a plentiful resource — after all, much of the Earth's surface is covered in it. But although there's lots of water around, most of it is not suitable for drinking (see previous page). Ninety-seven percent is salt water. Of the 3% that is fresh water, most of that is frozen, leaving less than 1% available for drinking purposes. And of that, only a fraction is easily accessible. So potential sources of drinking water are limited and not always accessible resources. They are also shrinking as more and more sources become too polluted to be used for drinking water, or salt water contaminates fresh water supplies. Limited water supplies are an important issue in many parts of the world, for example the Middle East and California.

We are also becoming more aware of it in the UK because of the number of recent droughts, the 1995/96 one being especially strong in our memory, when water was transported by lorry over the Pennines to Yorkshire, street standpipes were in evidence and hosepipe bans were commonplace.

Water is also a recycled resource (see the diagram of the hydrological cycle on page 14). There are three major reservoirs of water — atmospheric, land and oceanic — and water constantly cycles from one to another. When water falls to earth as rain, approximately 10% filters through the ground, 20% runs into lakes, rivers and oceans, and 70% returns to the atmosphere through evaporation and transpiration. But the water in the ground eventually filters into the lakes and rivers, lakes and rivers flow to the ocean, and water in lakes, rivers and oceans evaporates into the atmosphere, where it condenses to form clouds. The cycle is complete when it falls back to earth as rain.

Since rainfall replenishes the water resources on earth, it ultimately determines how much water is available for drinking. In the UK, the average annual rainfall is 1,050 mm per year, just slightly above the global average. However it varies considerably from region to region — the highest being in the uplands of Wales, Scotland and the Lake District (2,400 mm per year), the lowest being in the Thames estuary (500 mm per year). Ironically, it is the most populated areas, such as the south east, which need the most water and get the least rainfall.

Drinking water comes mainly from two sources: surface water and groundwater. Surface water consists of lakes, reservoirs, rivers and streams. It is the predominant source of drinking water in the north and west of England, and in Wales, Scotland and Northern Ireland. Groundwater is water trapped beneath the Earth's surface in porous, water-bearing rocks called aquifers. It is abstracted through wells and boreholes.

There are major limestone and sandstone aquifers over much of

England, but not in the west or in Wales. Roughly two thirds of the UK's water supply comes from surface water, and one third from groundwater sources.

Chapter 2

What's in it?

Drinking Water Characteristics

Chemically speaking, water consists of two molecules of hydrogen and one molecule of oxygen. Pure, distilled water is just that — hydrogen and oxygen. It's odourless and tasteless and not very pleasant to drink. But the water you find in nature is not pure H_2O — there's lots of other things in there too. It can contain dissolved minerals and gases and suspended particles. It can be hard or soft, acidic or alkaline, clear or cloudy. It may contain lots of organic material or none at all, and there may or may not be micro-organisms present.

All these natural characteristics determine the overall quality of the water: how good it tastes, how clean it looks, and how safe it is to drink. These characteristics vary from source to source and from day to day. Water suppliers have to consider these characteristics when deciding how to treat the water.

Dissolved Minerals

There are lots of minerals in soil that can dissolve in the water as it passes through, and they contribute to the taste of water. Some mineral-rich waters are bottled and sold as 'mineral water'.

The most common minerals found in water are ions of calcium, magnesium, sodium, bicarbonate, sulphate and chloride, iron, manganese, silica, nitrate, fluoride and various trace elements. Some of these elements are necessary for health (although we get most of our mineral requirements from food). Some create problems — too much iron or manganese, for example, will stain laundry and porcelain fixtures brown. Others, such as lead, mercury and cadmium, are toxic. Total dissolved solids in natural waters can range from 10 mg/l to over 100,000 mg/l, but if the concentration is higher than 500 mg/l, the water often has an unpleasantly strong taste.

Dissolved Gases

When surface water mixes with air, gases become dissolved. The most common dissolved gases are oxygen, nitrogen and carbon dioxide. They add to the quality of drinking water — without dissolved gases, water tastes 'flat'. Some groundwater supplies have enough dissolved carbon dioxide that the water is actually fizzy.

Suspended Particles

Suspended particles make the water appear cloudy or muddy. Technically, this is called turbidity. It can be caused by inorganic material such as mineral sediments or iron oxides, or organic material such as algae. Surface supplies become particularly turbid after a rainfall, when lots of soil particles wash into the water. Suspended particles are taken out during water treatment.

Colour

Colour is usually due to one of two things: organic material leaching from peat and other decaying vegetation, or metallic salts of iron and manganese. These are relatively harmless, but they can stain clothing and porcelain. Colour often changes during the year — in autumn, for example, water tends to be more coloured because surface waters are filled with decaying leaves.

Taste and Smell

Many things can give water unpleasant tastes and odours. Algae and moulds create a musty taste; iron, manganese and sulphates cause bitter tastes; hydrogen sulphide (produced by certain kinds of bacteria) has a characteristic rotten-egg smell, and chlorine residuals give water a chlorine taste, like water in a public

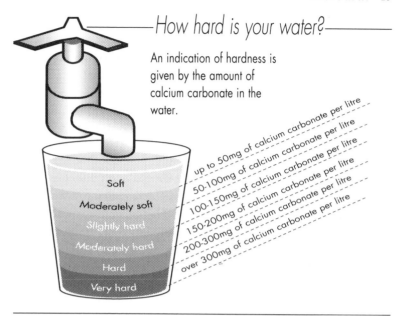

How hard is your water?

An indication of hardness is given by the amount of calcium carbonate in the water.

Soft — up to 50mg of calcium carbonate per litre

Moderately soft — 50-100mg of calcium carbonate per litre

Slightly hard — 100-150mg of calcium carbonate per litre

Moderately hard — 150-200mg of calcium carbonate per litre

Hard — 200-300mg of calcium carbonate per litre

Very hard — over 300mg of calcium carbonate per litre

swimming pool. Water treatment plants should remove most objectionable tastes and odours, but they are sometimes responsible for adding chlorine tastes, particularly if the chlorine reacts with other chemicals in the water. Many natural minerals can give a pleasant taste and odour, which is why people buy bottled mineral water.

Hardness

Dissolved calcium and magnesium salts, as well as strontium, iron and manganese cause hardness (see above). Hard water is good to drink, but too much hardness causes a couple of problems. One is scum: calcium can combine with fatty acids in soap to form scum on sinks, bathtubs and clothing, making washing difficult. The other is scale: both calcium and magnesium can combine with bicarbonates, carbonates, chlorides, nitrates, sulphate and silica in the water to form hard deposits in pipes and kettles. (See 'Making It Drinkable' for a discussion of water softeners.)

In contrast, softness is caused by high levels of carbonate and bicarbonate. Soft water is better for washing, but it is not so healthy to drink. It is linked to heart disease, and it can corrode lead pipes, increasing the level of lead in your drinking water. So water suppliers have to strike a balance and provide water soft enough to use for washing but hard enough to be healthy. UK regulations call for a minimum hardness of 60 mg of calcium per litre.

pH

pH describes how acidic or basic (see glossary) a sample of water is, measured on a scale from one to fourteen. Water with a pH lower than seven is defined as acidic; water with a pH higher than 7 is basic. Ideally, drinking water should be slightly basic, and treatment plants are required to keep pH between 6.5 and 8.5.

Acidity is usually the result either of carbon dioxide dissolving to produce weak carbonic acid, or of organic acids produced when leaves and other vegetation decompose. Water with a pH less than 6.5 can cause corrosion in metal pipes, increasing the metal content of your drinking water. Surface waters from peaty moorlands may have a pH as low as four.

Water with a pH above 8.5 will have a strong caustic taste and cause scale formation in pipes. Hard groundwater that has percolated through chalk or limestone can have a pH as high as 9.

Drinking Water Contamination

So natural characteristics contribute to the quality of water, making it good to drink, or bad to drink. But there are other things that get into water that also affect its quality. These are contaminants — any undesirable physical, chemical or microbiological substance. They find their way into water through a variety of processes, including run-off, leaching, effluent, and precipitation.

Run-off is water that travels over the surface of the land, picking up contaminants along the way. Urban run-off can contain lots of undesirable things: dirt and grit, dog faeces, disease-causing micro-organisms, heavy metals, pesticides, rubber particles from automobile tyres, and petrol and oil from leaking tanks. Agricultural run-off also causes significant pollution because it can contain large quantities of pesticides, fertilisers and animal wastes.

Leaching occurs when water percolates through a material — such as the soil — carrying dissolved substances into water courses. It is particularly dangerous when contaminants leach into groundwater, partly because the micro-organisms that help to

──────Care with household hazardous waste──────

Avoid putting chemicals down the drain! What you put down there can harm the aquatic environment, it can interfere with sewage treatment, and it can turn up in your drinking water. Motor oil, paints and solvents should particularly never go down the drain. Many local authorities have special facilities to deal with this kind of household hazardous waste — give your local environmental health officer a call. Old or unused drugs should be returned to your chemist, not flushed down the loo. Even many cleaning products are harmful, like washing powders, floor cleaners, oven cleaners and bleach. Make sure you use only safe, biodegradable alternatives — read the labels!

cleanse surface water do not live underground. Once groundwater becomes contaminated, it is very difficult to undo the damage. Common sources of groundwater pollution include leaking from cess pools, leachate from waste dumps, sewage lagoons, industrial lagoons, and landfills, as well as accidental spills, leaking underground storage tanks, mining, agriculture, and the movement of polluted surface water into underground supplies.

Effluent is more or less polluted water discharged into lakes, rivers and oceans, and it is the major source of surface water pollution. Sewage effluent is a major polluter, but industrial and agricultural effluent and acid drainage from coal and metal mines also contribute to poor water quality.

Precipitation can be another source of pollution in areas with poor air quality. When rain or snow falls through polluted air, it can pick up a whole host of contaminants including pesticides, asbestos dust, lead, chlorinated hydrocarbons, carbon monoxide, sulphur dioxide (the major cause of acid rain) nitrous oxides, and radioactive fallout.

Since water is constantly recycled between the atmosphere, the soils and the oceans, pollution that contaminates one part of the water cycle can eventually affect the entire system. Natural purification processes and water treatment plants help to cleanse water, but they can't take out everything. So what we dump down our drains can ultimately come back to us in our taps.

The majority of contaminants are not harmful. Some create bad

─────────────── *Measuring contaminants* ───────────────

Contaminants get into surface water from:

| Effluent | Leaching | Rainwater | Run-off |

Contaminants are usually present in extremely small quantities — so small that until recently, they couldn't be measured. Most contaminants are measured in units of milligrams (one thousandth of a gram) per litre of water (mg/l) or micrograms (one millionth of a gram) per litre of water (µg/l). One microgram of contaminant per litre means one part per million. One microgram per litre is even smaller: one part per billion.

───

tastes or odours, others can stain clothing and fixtures, while most have no effect. There are a few dangerous contaminants, however, and these must be monitored closely.

In the nineteenth century, the biggest threat to drinking water supplies was from bacteria and viruses that caused disease. When untreated sewage contaminated drinking water supplies in London, hundreds of thousands of people died from typhoid and cholera. Today, modern water treatment methods have eliminated all but a few water-borne diseases in developed countries, and now the focus of concern has shifted to the possible long-term effects of small quantities of chemical contaminants.

Major Contaminants

The following is a list of common contaminants in your drinking water that may be of concern. It describes where they come from, what they're likely to do to you, how they can be removed, and what UK regulations say are acceptable levels. These are only a handful of the contaminants that can be present in your drinking water, but they are some of the more important ones.

It's worth mentioning that the jury is still out on the health effects of many of these substances. One study may show a

——Deciding which chemicals cause cancer——

When the World Health Organisation tries to decide which chemicals cause cancer in humans, it looks at two kinds of evidence: studies of cancer in human populations ('epidemiological evidence') and experimental research on laboratory animals. Both types of evidence have their weaknesses. When it comes to epidemiological studies, it's easy to say that a particular group of people has a higher risk of cancer, but it's difficult to say what causes that risk, especially because cancers take many years to develop. When it comes to animal studies, the problem is that it's not always possible to say that something that causes cancer in guinea pigs when it's fed to them in large doses for a short period of time will cause cancer to humans in small doses over long periods of time. The WHO weighs all the evidence and then classifies chemicals into four groups, according to the following criteria:

Group 1 chemicals cause cancer. Something is classified as group 1 if there is sufficient evidence that it causes cancer in humans.

Group 2 chemicals may cause cancer.
Group 2A chemicals probably cause cancer, based on limited evidence in humans or sufficient evidence in animals.
Group 2B chemicals possibly cause cancer, based on limited evidence in humans or less than sufficient evidence in animals.

Group 3 chemicals are substances that can't be classified because there is not enough evidence in humans or animals.

Group 4 chemicals probably don't cause cancer. Something is classified as group 4 if the evidence suggests it doesn't cause cancer in humans or animals.

---

substance is linked to cancer in humans, another may not. The problem is finding good evidence (see the box above) It's also important to mention that children tend to be more susceptible to dangerous contaminants than adults because their immune systems are not as strong and they consume more, per kilogram of body weight, than adults.

————*Case study: Groundwater contamination*————

in Coventry and Birmingham

Industrial solvents are a major cause of groundwater contamination. This is a particularly big problem in the heavily industrialised cities of Coventry and Birmingham. In Coventry, nearly all drinking water boreholes and industrial boreholes have total solvent concentrations over 10 µg/l. In Birmingham, solvent and metal contamination is bad enough that groundwater is no longer used as a source for drinking water. Thirty percent of wells have more than 100 µg/l of trichloroethylene, a common industrial solvent.

To make the situation worse, the groundwater level is rising in Birmingham. As it rises, the water is coming in contact with highly polluted soil, increasing the degree of groundwater pollution. Unfortunately, this is a long term problem. Solvents take a long time to percolate into groundwater, so the problems we face today were created decades ago.

Aluminium
Health effects

There's lots of talk about a connection between aluminium and Alzheimer's disease. Although Alzheimer's patients have high levels of aluminium in their brains, at the moment it isn't clear whether this is a cause of the disease or just an effect. A Medical Research Council study found the risk of Alzheimer's was 1.5 times higher in districts where average aluminium concentrations were more than 0.11 mg/l than in regions where the concentrations were below 0.01 mg/l. However, a recent Department of Health study concluded there was not enough evidence to establish a definite connection. If there isn't a history of Alzheimer's disease in your family, you probably don't need to worry about how much aluminium you ingest. But if you have a relative who has Alzheimer's, you may want to reduce your consumption. You could stop using aluminium cookware, and not drink large quantities of tea. However, more aluminium occurs in other foods such as bread, and indigestion tablets (especially those ending in "-al") than could be ingested from cooking in aluminium pans or drinking from aluminium cans, according to the Alzheimer's Society.

Source

Aluminium occurs naturally in water. As aluminium is the second most common element in the Earth's rocks, it is present in many soils, and can migrate into waters that come into contact with those soils. It is particularly common in acidic surface waters from upland areas such as moors. However, the biggest source of aluminium in drinking water is from aluminium sulphate used during the water treatment process as a coagulant that removes colour and turbidity from drinking water. If it is not completely removed, there will be high levels of aluminium in your drinking water.

Acceptable levels

UK regulations set a limit of 200 µg of aluminium per litre of drinking water. However, the amount of aluminium you get from your drinking water is probably only 5% of your average daily intake.

Treatment

Aluminium can be removed by sedimentation and filtration (see 'Water Treatment Plants').

Lead

Health effects

Lead is probably the most dangerous contaminant in UK drinking water. It is a poison that accumulates in the body and affects the nervous system, causing mental retardation and behavioural problems in young children, and increasing the risk of still births and low birth-weight babies. It can also cause anaemia.

Source

Most lead contamination in drinking water is due to lead in household pipes. Many houses built before 1976 have lead in the household plumbing or in the pipes connecting them to the mains. It is also present in solder used to join copper pipes. Lead contamination from plumbing happens mainly in areas where the water is soft and acidic, but it can also occur in hard water areas. The Water Research Centre (WRc) estimates that 8.9 million homes in England and Wales have lead plumbing. General geographical areas with

Worried about Lead?

Checking Your Home for Lead Pipework

There are two simple checks to find out if your water plumbing is lead. An unpainted lead pipe is dull grey and soft. If you scrape the surface gently with a knife, you will see the dull (shiny if scratched), soft, silver coloured metal beneath.

1. Look in or behind cupboards in your kitchen. Locate the pipe leading to the kitchen tap. Check as much of the pipe as possible.
2. Locate the stop valve outside your property. Examine, where possible, the piping from the stop valve to your property.

Pipes may also be;

copper — bright, hard and dull brown.

iron — dark, very hard and may be rusty.

plastic — may be grey, black or blue.

Removing Lead Pipework

All the plumbing inside your home to the kitchen tap is your responsibility or your landlord's. If you have any lead pipework between the stop valve outside your home and the kitchen tap, remove it and replace it with plastic or copper pipework. Grants are available for renovation and minor works for households with a low income. Contact your local authority for further information about this.

Further Advice

If you have any further doubts or queries concerning lead piping, information can be obtained from your water supplier, your <$iLocal Authority> Environmental Health Officer, or a qualified plumber, such as one registered with the Institute of Plumbing.

---

lead distribution pipes include north, south and west Wales, the Midlands, Lincolnshire, Oxfordshire, Cambridgeshire, Middlesex, Lancashire, Scotland and Northern Ireland. If you are concerned, check with your supplier for more specific information.

Acceptable levels

EC regulations and UK regulations both set a limit of 50 µg/l of lead in drinking water. However, this standard applies to different points in the system. The EC sets the limit for the water that comes out of your tap, making sure that the water you drink doesn't contain more than 50 µg/l; but the UK regulations set the limit at the point where the water passes from the water supplier's pipe into your service pipe. This means that if your household plumbing contains lead pipes, the water that comes out of your tap may have more than 50 µg/l of lead. If there is a risk of 50 µg/l being exceeded at your tap, water suppliers are supposed to treat the water to reduce the risk — for example, by keeping the pH of the water between 8.0 and 8.5 — but this doesn't guarantee that your tap water won't have high levels of lead. Three percent of samples exceeded standards in England and Wales in 1991; 4% exceeded standards in Scotland in 1992.

The World Health Organisation's standards for lead in drinking water are much stricter than EC standards: it sets a limit of 10 µg/l. This is a much safer level for foetuses and young children. The Ministry of Agriculture, Fisheries and Food recommends that bottle-fed infants should not be given water with lead levels greater than 10 to 15 µg/l.

Treatment

If you suspect lead in your tap water, the first thing to do is to follow the advice on the previous page. Many authorities will inspect your plumbing and check the amount of lead in your tap water free of charge. Ideally, if a problem exists, you should replace the plumbing. Unfortunately, water authorities aren't responsible for the condition of pipes within the boundary of your property, so you'll have to foot the bill for new plumbing yourself, but you may be able to get a grant from your local council to help with the cost. If you replace the lead pipes in your house, your water supplier is obliged to replace its section of the lead service pipe.

The Water Research Centre believes it is necessary to remove completely lead pipes to meet the 10 µg/l limit. It estimates there are 8.9 million properties in England and Wales that have at least some lead plumbing, and the Scottish Agency estimates there are 600,000 homes in Scotland with lead pipes.

If replacing the pipes isn't possible, you should run the taps for

─────────*Abandoned Mine Discharges*─────────

When mines are abandoned and the pumps that prevent them from filling with water are turned off, groundwater levels will rise and flush iron and other metals out of the mines and into local rivers and streams. For example, the River Rhymney in South Wales fills with orange-coloured sludge each summer because of high iron content from the coalfields, and metal-filled water from the Wheal Jane tin mine in Cornwall discolours the Carrick Roads estuary. This iron sludge can spoil several kilometres of river, disrupting its ecology by settling out on the river bottom and smothering the invertebrates that live there.

The National Rivers Authority reports there are over 90 km of waterways in England and Wales affected by abandoned coal mines, and 180 km affected by abandoned metal mines. Currently it is not an offence to pollute water by permitting water from an abandoned mine to enter controlled water, according to UK water pollution legislation.

---

several minutes before using the water for drinking or cooking, particularly in the morning when the water has been sitting in the pipes overnight. Some jug filters will take out lead — the Waymaster Crystal, for example. See 'Filter Systems' for details.

Nitrates

Nitrates are molecules that occur naturally and are necessary for plants to grow. They are a major component of fertilisers. If too much nitrate gets into a lake, a process known as 'eutrophication', it can cause massive blooms of algae.

Health effects

These are relatively few and far between. Nitrates have had a lot of bad press but this is largely due to the pollution of streams and rivers by agricultural run-off. Occasionally, nitrates are connected with 'blue baby syndrome', a condition where a baby's red blood cells can't carry enough oxygen to the body. The baby becomes starved of oxygen and turns blue. However, most cases of blue baby syndrome are due to other causes. In the UK there have been only 14 cases in the past 42 years that were caused by nitrates in drinking water — the last confirmed case was in 1972. Those at most risk are infants fed on formula milk made with water from a well with a high nitrate contamination level. There may also be a connection between nitrites (about a 1/4 of nitrates are broken down in the body into nitrites) and stomach cancer. When nitrites react with certain foods, they may produce nitrosamines, which are able to cause cancer. However there is little epidemiological evidence to support this occurance of cancer in humans by this means.

Source

Nitrate in drinking water can come from two sources. Nitrate is produced naturally when ammonia breaks down, but this is only a small percentage of the nitrate found in drinking water. By far the biggest source of nitrate in drinking water is chemical fertilisers. Much of the groundwater and surface water supplies in the UK are contaminated by agricultural run-off containing quick-release nitrogen fertilisers. Also, because the use of these fertilisers has substantially increased in the last two decades, the levels of nitrate in our drinking water will continue to rise as they slowly move down through the soil into our groundwater supplies. Nitrate levels are particularly high in the intensive agricultural areas of East Anglia, the Severn and the Trent.

Acceptable levels

EC and UK regulations set a maximum level of 50 mg per litre. If your drinking water contains less than 10 mg/l, vegetables will probably be your major source of nitrate. On the other hand, if the nitrate level in your water is 50 mg/l, most of your nitrate intake will be from drinking water. Some people believe these standards are not realistic, since many areas in Europe are having difficulty meeting them. Others say strict standards are important to protect our health, and farmers must change the way they use fertilisers so the standards can be met. If they did it would also improve the rivers and soils.

Treatment

There is no cheap or simple way to reduce nitrate concentrations, except by mixing contaminated water with clean supplies. Specialised treatment such as ion exchange and denitrifying bacteria can be used, but these are much more costly options. Leaving water a long time in reservoirs can help. Some water companies in areas at risk offer bottled water to consumers instead.

Trihalomethanes (THMs)

Trihalomethanes are a type of organic molecule containing one carbon atom, one hydrogen atom and three halogen atoms; they include chloroform trichloromethane, ($CHCL_3$), bromodichloromethane ($CHCL_2Br$), dibromochloromethane ($CHCLBr_2$), and tribromomethane ($CHBr_3$).

Health effects

According to the World Health Organisation, chloroform and bromodichloromethane are 'possible' carcinogens. It says if you drink 1 litre a day at 30µg/l you have a 1 in 100,000 risk of developing cancer.

Source

As leaves and other vegetation in surface water break down, they release certain organic substances. So do nitrate-rich, low-flow rivers in places of intensive agriculture. THMs are formed when chlorine reacts with these substances. This means that if chlorine is used to disinfect water that contains high levels of organic substances, THMs may be formed. Because chlorine is the most common disinfectant used in water treatment, THMs are a serious concern in drinking water.

Treatment

There are two basic approaches to solving this problem: preventing THMs from forming in the first place, or take them out once they've been formed. In areas at risk water suppliers can prevent THMs from forming by settling out, coagulating or filtering the organic material in the water before they disinfect it, so there are fewer organic precursors to form THMs when they add chlorine. They can use non-chlorine disinfectants such as ultraviolet radiation and ozonation. Alternatively, activated carbon can be used to remove THMs after they have been formed. However, it is important not to compromise disinfection in lowering the level of THMs — the health risk of not disinfecting properly is much greater than the health risk of consuming THMs.

Acceptable levels

According to UK regulations, the concentrations of the four THMs combined cannot be more than 100 µg/l. There are no EC regulations concerning this, but the German level is 25μg/l and the US one 50μg/l. There is concern that British standards are too lax.

Polycyclic Aromatic Hydrocarbons (PAHs)

These are synthetic compounds with a molecular structure containing two or more benzene rings, derived from coal and oil product.

Health effects

Some PAHs cause tumours in mice. The World Health Organisation classifies them as 'probable' carcinogens. They are readily absorbed in the body and stored in fat tissue.

Source

PAHs occur in soot, vehicle exhausts, tar and tar products. Run-off from roads may be a source in the original supply. They can find their way into drinking water if the treated water travels through old iron mains lined with an internal anti-corrosion coating of coal tar pitch (common in pipes laid before the mid 1970s). You can ask your water supplier if mains lined with coal tar pitch are used in your area.

Acceptable levels

The EC maximum admissible concentration for the total of six specified PAHs is 0.2 μg/l. However, the amount of PAHs you get from drinking water is small compared to what you get from food and cigarette smoke.

Treatment

PAHs are usually removed during the water treatment process by coagulation, sedimentation and filtration (see 'Water Treatment Plants'). However they can be re-introduced if the treated water is distributed in older mains still lined with coal tar pitch.

Pesticides

Pesticides are chemicals that kill pests. These include herbicides, which kill weeds; insecticides, which kill insects; and fungicides, which kill moulds and fungi. They are widely used on farmland, roadside verges, parks, golf courses and private gardens, and they find their way into water sources in large quantities. There are approximately 450 active pesticide ingredients used in the UK. Of greatest concern are the insecticides chlorodine,

—————Pesticides and breast cancer—————

Most breast cancer is due to high levels of the female hormone oestrogen. The more oestrogen you are exposed to over your lifetime, the higher the risk that you will develop breast cancer. So the sooner you enter puberty and the later you enter menopause, the more oestrogen you are exposed to. Also, the more fat tissue you have, the more oestrogen you are exposed to, because fat cells produce oestrogen.

It is now becoming clear that certain chemicals, including pesticides, can mimic the effects of oestrogen. So exposure to certain pesticides could increase the risk of breast cancer. Atrazine, a common pesticide in the UK, is the most recently identified oestrogenic compound. Although the Ministry of Agriculture's Advisory Committee on Pesticides concluded that the levels of atrazine found in drinking water were "not of toxicological significance to humans", atrazine is just one of a growing list of oestrogenic substances found in our drinking water.

coumaphor, umethoate and phorate and triazophous. The WHO guide value is 2µg/l. Eastern and southern England have the most problems.

Health effects

Since there are so many different types of pesticides, it is difficult to list all the health effects. Many are possible carcinogens. Little is known about the long-term effects of drinking low levels. There have been suggestions of links to breast cancer (see the box above).

Source

Chemicals have been used as a significant form of pest control since 1945. Today there is almost no agricultural area in the world that does not use pesticides.

Acceptable levels

The amount of pesticide you are exposed to annually in your drinking water is rarely a health risk, but there can be dangerous seasonal peaks when pesticide applications run off into local watercourses or seep into groundwater. UK regulations set a limit of 0.1 µg/l for individual pesticides and 0.5 µg/l for total pesticide levels. These limits are frequently exceeded. Almost 15% of

————————— *Pesticide contamination*—————————

- in untreated groundwater, 1992

atrazine	9% of samples exceeded UK limits of 0.1 µg/l
terbutryn	4%
trietazine	3%
isoproturon	2%

- in untreated surface water 1992

atrazine	17% of samples exceeded UK limits of 0.1 µg/l
mecoprop	17%
2,4D	15%
diuron	14%
simazine	13%
isoproturon	10%
permethrin	6%
pentachlorophenol	6%
dicamba	5%
sulcofuron	5%
chlortoluron	4%

n.b. Bentazone is also a common contaminant of groundwaters and surface waters, but the National Rivers Authority did not begin testing for it until quite recently.

Source: *UK Environment, Department of Environment*

groundwaters and 8% of surface waters are contaminated with bentazone. Atrazine, simazine, 2,4D and mecoprop are also common drinking water contaminants. Even DDT occasionally turns up, although it was banned from use several decades ago. However, unless you eat organically grown foods grown without pesticides, the amount of pesticide you get from your drinking water is only a small fraction of the amount you consume in your food.

Hormonal contamination

It now seems that contaminants in sewage can act like the female hormone oestrogen. In 1992, male fish close to a major sewage outfall on the Lea River in Hertfordshire were discovered producing vitellogenin, a yolk protein normally produced only in fertile females. More recently, male fish in the River Aire in West Yorkshire were discovered with stunted testicles and vitellogenin proteins.

Both these effects are believed to be due to alkylphenols, detergent by-products that mimic the effects of oestrogen. A follow up study by the Ministry of Agriculture's Directorate of Fisheries Research and by Brunel University found that many rivers are contaminated with these chemicals. So far, there does not seem to be any immediate risk to human health, since tap water has not caused any oestrogenic effects in fish. The Soap and Detergent Industries Association has pledged its members will phase out the dangerous chemicals by 1997.

Treatment

Pesticide levels can be reduced by activated carbon adsorption or ozonation (see 'Water Treatment Plants'), but some still turn up in drinking water. You can remove pesticides from your tap water by using a jug filter or an in-line filter with activated carbon (see 'Filter Systems' and 'Making It Drinkable').

Pathogens

Pathogens are any viruses, bacteria; health threat bacteria or other micro-organisms that can cause disease.

Health effects

There are a whole host of diseases caused by water-borne pathogens. These include cholera, typhoid fever, bacillary dysentery, amoebic dysentery, cryptosporidiosis, giardiasis, poliomyelitis, infectious hepatitis, and schistosomiasis. Some particularly worrisome pathogens are described separately below.

Source

Pathogens can be transmitted by human or animal faeces. Whenever sewage contaminates a water supply, there is a danger that pathogens could be present.

—————Case study: Cryptosporidiosis outbreak—————

In 1988/89, a large outbreak of cryptosporidiosis occurred in Swindon and parts of Oxfordshire. The first cases occurred in December 1988 and the outbreak peaked in February and March 1989. In total, 500 cases were confirmed by laboratory tests and it is likely that around 5,000 people were actually affected. The outbreak was probably caused by faeces from infected cows washing into the River Windrush. In November '88, cattle grazing next to the Windrush had severe diarrhoea, suggesting they had cryptosporidiosis. Coincidentally, the river flow was exceptionally low due to unusually warm weather. The combination of high levels of oocysts and low quantities of water was more than the treatment system could deal with effectively. The outbreak prompted the Government to set up an expert committee and a cryptosporidium research and monitoring programme costing £2 million.

Acceptable levels

As it would be too difficult and too expensive to test for all possible pathogens, water suppliers test for coliform bacteria instead, because they are naturally present in human and animal faeces. So if there are coliforms in the water, it means the water has been contaminated with sewage, and therefore other pathogens may be present. According to UK regulations, no 100ml sample of treated water is allowed to contain any coliforms.

Treatment

Disinfection will remove most pathogens (see 'Water Treatment Plants'), but not all. See specific examples below.

Cryptosporidium

Health effects

Cryptosporidium is a parasite that causes acute cases of diarrhoea lasting two to three weeks. There is no effective treatment for this disease. It is transmitted by oocysts, a highly resistant form of the parasite. People exposed to low levels of the oocyst can build up an immunity to it. In healthy individuals cryptosporidiosis is unpleasant, but it is not particularly dangerous and will go away without treatment. However, in people with low immunity, such as people with AIDS, it is very serious and can be fatal. *AIDS Treatment Update* recommends that anyone with a T-cell count below 200 should boil water to inactivate the oocysts before using it for drinking or for washing food. Cryptosporidiosis is the sixth commonest cause of diarrhoea in the UK.

Source

Oocysts are excreted in the faeces of infected hosts. Most cryptosporidium oocysts originate from infected livestock.

Acceptable levels

Presently there are no standards for acceptable levels of cryptosporidium oocysts. Coliforms are not an adequate indicator for the presence of oocysts, because oocysts are far more resistant to disinfection than coliforms.

Treatment

Water treatment plants can deal with low levels of oocysts, but if the concentration becomes too high, some oocysts will pass into the drinking water supply. Chlorine has no effect.

Giardia
Health effects

Giardia is a parasite that causes diarrhoea and fever.

Source

Like cryptosporidium, it is found in the faeces of infected animals in the form of small, resilient cysts.

Acceptable levels

No acceptable levels have been established for giardia, but, as in the case of cryptosporidium, coliforms are not a good indicator for the presence of cysts. A Scottish study found cysts in 40% of untreated water sources and in 20% of treated supplies. These results suggest that water treatment does not adequately remove giardia cysts and that giardia contamination may be widespread in UK water supplies.

Treatment

Over 99.7% of cysts are removed by slow sand filtration, or by coagulation followed by rapid gravity filtration. A smaller percentage is removed by micro-straining (see 'Water Treatment Plants'). They are more susceptible to disinfection than cryptosporidium.

——————How pure is your water?——————

Percentage of water supply zones complying with standards, 1993. Pesticides and iron are clearly the trickiest of contaminants to eradicate. (Water supply zones are local geographic areas that supply up to 50,000 people.)

coliforms	98.9%
faecal coliforms	93.6%
colour	99.3%
turbidity	96.1%
odour	99.3%
taste	98.9%
pH	94.3%
nitrate	98.0%
nitrite	90.5%
aluminium	94.6%
iron	74.0%
manganese	93.1%
lead	79.1%
PAH	89.9%
THM	98.6%
total pesticides	88.1%
individual pesticides	72.1%

Wholesome Water

Under the 1991 Water Industry Act, UK water suppliers have a duty to provide consumers with 'wholesome water' for drinking, washing and cooking. Water is considered wholesome if the levels of contaminants do not exceed standards set by UK regulations and its taste, odour, clarity and colour are acceptable. The complete standards are listed in the appendix. Most water supplies do meet these standards (see previous page).

However, the fact that water meets standards does not always mean there are not harmful levels of contaminants in it. Setting maximum acceptable levels is an extremely difficult business for many contaminants. Ideally, standards should be based on documented health effects of long-term exposure, but as discussed earlier, the data is often insufficient or contradictory. Sometimes standards are entirely arbitrary. For example, at the time they were established, EC standards for pesticides were based on the lowest detectable limit, not on any documented health effects from consuming that amount of pesticide. This means the EC pesticide standards are much stricter than standards set by the World Health Organisation.

It is also impossible to set standards for all the different chemicals that might get into water supplies. New chemicals are being developed at an astounding rate. There are now approximately 70,000 chemicals in use and 500 to 1,000 added each year. We don't know what the long-term effects of many of these chemicals are, nor do we know what happens when they combine with each other.

So despite all the regulations and tests, 'wholesome' water does not necessarily guarantee safe water.

Chapter Three

How is it treated?

Although water can be contaminated, both by natural processes and through human action, it can also be cleansed. Some purification occurs naturally, as water percolates through soil or travels down a stream. However, these processes do not usually create drinking-quality water. For this to be achieved on a larger scale, water treatment plants are required.

The Natural Cleansing Processes

As groundwater seeps through the earth to underground layers of water-bearing rock called aquifers, contaminants are naturally filtered out. How much gets removed depends on how thick a layer of earth the water passes through and what that layer is made of. Clay is the most effective at filtering water, but silt and sand are also good if they are sufficiently fine grained and form a thick enough layer. There are also living organisms in the soil that break down organic contaminants, and any pathogens that do make it into groundwater supplies don't tend to survive — conditions in aquifers are not very hospitable to micro-organisms.

Purification also takes place in surface water, but for different reasons. There are many micro-organisms naturally present in the water that feed on organic contaminants and break them down. There are no processes that occur in surface water to remove suspended particles, but sunlight helps to kill off harmful, disease-causing bacteria and viruses.

—————————*Surface water treatment*—————————

In this typical surface water treatment plant, water goes through several stages before it is ready for drinking. The complete process takes several hours.

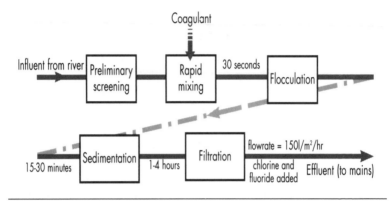

Water Treatment Plants

The purpose of a municipal water treatment plant is to provide water that tastes reasonable and is safe to drink, as well as water of adequate quality for industrial uses. To accomplish this, treatment plants use a variety of processes to cleanse and purify water. Which particular ones are used depends on the quality of the raw incoming water, and the treatment plant must be flexible enough to deal with daily and seasonal changes in the raw water quality. Generally, surface water requires more treatment than groundwater because it tends to be more contaminated (see diagram above.) The standard processes are described below.

There are also a number of specialised and advanced water treatment processes. Among others, these include softening hard water, and removing iron, manganese and objectionable tastes and odours. Water may also be fluoridated if natural fluoride levels are low (see 'The Fluoride Issue' below) or defluoridated if natural levels are too high.

Preliminary Screening and Straining

Screening and straining are not necessary for groundwater, but they are important for removing suspended solids from surface

The Camelford Incident

On July 6 1988, 20,000 people in Cornwall were poisoned and 60,000 fish killed when large quantities of aluminium sulphate were accidentally discharged into the mains water supply. The incident took place in the Camelford area served by the Lowermoor water treatment plant. A relief tanker driver arrived to deliver 20 tonnes of aluminium sulphate and found the plant unstaffed. He mistakenly poured the 8% solution (6,000 times the EC maximum admissible concentration of aluminium) into the reservoir of treated water instead of the storage containers. The now highly acidic drinking water stripped metal from water pipes and tanks as it flowed through the distribution system, increasing copper and zinc up to 9000 µg/l and increasing lead levels fourfold. Seven thousand households were affected and residents suffered from acute metal poisoning and acid burns. When the South West Water Authority flushed the contaminated water out into the Camel and Allen rivers, 60,000 salmon and trout died as a result.

A Health Advisory Group was set up to investigate the incident. The report concluded it was unlikely there were any long term health effects that could be attributed to the incident, although some residents complain of joint and muscle pains, malaise, fatigue, and memory loss. A further investigation confirmed this conclusion.

The Camelford incident illustrates that human errors can occur in the treatment process and highlights the need for good procedures.

---

water. Screening removes the largest particles, such as leaves, twigs and rags. The screens can be vertical bars, rotating drums, or continuous strips of perforated material located at the water intake. They must be periodically jet washed or raked to remove debris. Micro-strainers are made of very fine stainless steel wire mesh designed to remove most suspended solids, including most plankton and algae.

Coagulation & Flocculation

These techniques are used to remove colour, turbidity and algae. Water suppliers add a chemical such as alum (hydrated

Slow gravity sand filtration

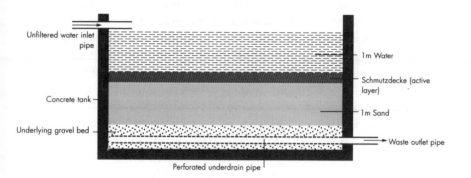

In a slow sand filter, the water is cleansed by the micro-organisms in the *schmutzdecke* and by the sand itself.

Rapid gravity sand filtration

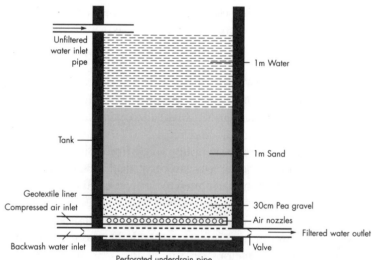

In a rapid gravity filter, the water is cleansed as it passes through the layer of sand. The sand must be aerated and backwashed frequently.

(This illustration, and all others in this book, is schematic, and not drawn to scale.)

aluminium sulphate) to the water. When alum reacts with water, it forms aluminium hydroxide, which is effectively positively charged. Most of the suspended particles are negatively charged, so they are attracted to the aluminium hydroxide and form clumps — or 'flocs'- trapping other impurities in the process. The flocs are easily separated from the water by sedimentation and filtration. Other common coagulants include sodium aluminate, ferrous sulphate and lime, and ferric chloride.

Sedimentation

Sedimentation (sometimes referred to as clarification) is the process of using gravity to settle flocs out of the water after coagulation and flocculation. It works best in slow moving or still water, so water suppliers use large settling tanks to reduce the speed of the water. Sedimentation can also be used on its own at the beginning of the treatment process to remove suspended solids in very cloudy water.

Coagulation, flocculation and sedimentation are relatively expensive processes that require large amounts of initial capital expenditure for the tanks and ongoing expenditures for chemicals and maintenance.

Filtration

Filtration is the process of passing water through beds of porous material to remove suspended particles. There are a large number of methods available; the two most commonly used are slow sand filtration and rapid gravity filtration.

Slow sand filtration uses layers of sand to filter the water. As the water moves through progressively finer sand, more contaminants are filtered out. Slow sand filters also have a biologically active 'schmutzdecke' (a German term meaning 'dirt layer'). This is a thin layer of inorganic and organic particles derived from the raw water that naturally develops on top of the sand as the water filters through (see diagram on page 42) and helps to break down organic particles in the water. Directly below this develops a thicker, autotropic layer containing many microorganisms that feed on organic contaminants and potentially pathogenic organisms. Slow sand filters are simple to operate and maintain. Every few months the system must be drained and the top few centimetres of sand removed when the *schmutzdecke* grows too thick. A slow sand filtration system can process approximately 150 litres of water per square metre per hour. Unlike other large-scale filtration systems, these filters can remove non-biodegradable detergents.

Rapid gravity filtration is similar to slow sand filtration, but it is much faster and can handle a flow rate of $4,000l/m^2/hr$. It is also cheaper to install and operate and it occupies less area. However, the sand particles in a rapid gravity filter aren't as fine as the ones in a slow sand filter and no *schmutzdecke* forms, so it's not as efficient at removing contaminants. The system must be backwashed daily and the sand particles separated using compressed air, so rapid gravity filtration requires more energy than slow sand filtration. Both methods remove nearly all bacteria, ammonium and odours, as well as many dissolved particles.

Disinfection

This is the most important and probably the most controversial step in the treatment process. The object is to kill or inactivate pathogens, including bacteria, amoebic cysts, algae, spores and viruses, making the water safe to drink.

The ideal disinfectant should be effective against all pathogens present in whatever quantity is there. It should leave a 'residual' — that is, some of it should still be present to continue to disinfect the water after it leaves the plant, protecting the water from possible recontamination as it travels to your tap. It should be cheap, reliable and easy to produce, and it should be fast and effective in a variety of water conditions. Finally, it should create no harmful by-products.

Unfortunately, no single disinfectant meets all these requirements. The most commonly used disinfectants are chlorine, chloramines, chlorine dioxide, ozone and <$iultraviolet irradiation. Their strengths and weaknesses are described below.

Chlorine

In 1881, Robert Koch first demonstrated that chlorine could kill bacteria. This knowledge was put to use in 1905, when continuous chlorination of a public water supply was used to combat typhoid epidemics in London. Since then, chlorine has become widely used as a water supply disinfectant.

Unfortunately, although it is effective at killing pathogens, chlorination creates by-products — chlorinated organic compounds — many of which cause cancer in laboratory animals. These include dioxins and PCBs, and are termed generally organochlorines, including cancer of the bladder, colon and rectum. In addition, several epidemiological studies have found connections between the presence of chlorine by-products in drinking water and increased rates of certain cancers in the humans drinking it. The Department of Health and Social Services' Committee on Medical Aspects of Air, Soil and Water does not believe chlorination by-products are dangerous. After examining the data it reported: "We have found no sound reason to conclude that the consumption of the by-products of chlorination, in drinking-water which has been treated and chlorinated according to current practices, increases the risk of cancer in humans." Still, there is doubt about the long term safety of chlorine disinfection for humans, and it certainly isn't good for fish.

Chlorine has a lot of practical strengths. It can be administered as a liquid or as a gas, it is effective against viruses and bacteria, and it leaves traces that continue to disinfect after the water has left the treatment plant. It is reliable, widely used and relatively cheap.

Greenpeace calls for a total global ban on chlorine use. It advocates instead the substitution of ozone or ultraviolet treatment of drinking water. However, this may actually increase overall health risks since only chlorine continues to prevent infection after treatment. In spite of this, many municipalities on the continent do not use chlorine. It is a question of balancing respective risks.

These arguments and considerations also apply to the use of chlorine in swimming pools.

Chlorine Dioxide

Since chlorine can create taste and odour problems, chlorine dioxide is often used as an alternative. It is effective at killing bacteria and viruses and it leaves a residual disinfectant. However, like chlorine, it produces harmful chlorinated by-products.

Chlorine dioxide must be generated on site by combining chlorine and sodium chlorite. It is widely used in Europe, but is not as common in the US. It is almost ten times as expensive as chlorine.

Chloramines

Chloramines are formed from chlorine and ammonia. They are moderately effective against bacteria, but not so good at killing viruses. Their advantage is that they produce a stronger residual disinfectant than chlorine. The specific by-products of chloramines are not known, but because they contain chlorine, they are potentially harmful. Chloramines are used widely in the US and cost roughly twice as much as chlorine.

Ozone

Ozone is generated on site by passing dry air or oxygen (O_2) through an electric charge, converting it to ozone (O_3). The ozone gas is then bubbled through the water. It is an excellent disinfectant for bacteria and viruses, eliminates tastes and odours, and breaks down pesticides. However, it does create a number of by-products, including bromates, formaldehyde and acetaldehyde, which has been shown to cause kidney tumours in rats and may cause cancer in humans. Ozone does not produce a residual disinfectant, so another disinfectant must be added to protect the treated water from recontamination. Furthermore, the equipment has proved to be relatively unreliable, requiring frequent and varied maintenance and repair. It is used widely in France and Canada and costs five times as much as chlorine.

Ultraviolet Irradiation

Ultraviolet (UV) radiation is generated by light bulbs which are immersed in the water. The UV rays work by damaging the genetic material in bacteria and viruses, preventing them from reproducing. The biggest advantage of UV irradiation is that it does not generate harmful by-products. Also, it requires minimal contact time and works independent of pH. However, it leaves no residual in the distribution system, so there is no sustained disinfection. UK treatment plants that use UV often add a small dose of chlorine for residual protection. The effectiveness of UV irradiation is reduced by suspended solids in the water, so it is important that the incoming water is cleaned well before it is disinfected. It is widely accepted as a disinfectant for private supplies and is now increasingly used for public supplies.

The Fluoride Issue

Fluoride protects teeth against cavities, up to a certain limit. The higher the level of fluoride you ingest, the fewer cavities you're likely to develop. It works by increasing the resistance of your tooth enamel to the acids produced by bacterial plaques. If fluoride levels are too high, however, dental fluorosis can occur. This is a condition where teeth become mottled and discoloured. In extreme cases the enamel becomes pitted. The optimal concentration of fluoride to maximise protection against cavities and minimise the risk of dental fluorosis is 1.0 mg/l. This is the rate at which it is currently added to water supplies, the concentration being carefully monitored on a daily or continuous basis. Early studies showed great benefit to fluoridation at this level, where water fluoridation reduced the prevalence of cavities by 40 to 50% in milk teeth and by 50 to 60% in adult teeth. However, more recent studies have shown little difference in tooth decay between communities with fluoridated water and communities without, but this is probably because of the widespread use of fluoridated toothpaste.

Most waters naturally contain some fluoride, but the concentration varies a lot depending on the water source. Some communities therefore supplement the natural levels by adding additional fluoride. The first community water fluoridation scheme was set up in the United States in 1945. In 1969, the World Health Organisation recommended that countries introduce community water fluoridation because it was (and still is) the least expensive and most effective way of providing fluoride to large numbers of people. Fluoridation in the UK began in the early 1960s. Currently, 12% of the population on piped water supply systems receive fluoridated water. To find out if your tap water is fluoridated contact your water supplier. Water suppliers are permitted to supplement the fluoride content of water supplies within a specified area at the written request of a Health Authority.

Many people object to authorities adding substances to their drinking water. They point out that community fluoridation is not the only way to administer fluoride — individuals can use fluoride tablets to treat their own water if they want fluoridated water. Most toothpaste now contains fluoride. In contrast, it is much more difficult for people to remove fluoride from the water supply once it's been put in. It cannot be boiled out or filtered out.

Its use has been rejected by 13 European countries. By fluoridating public water supplies, authorities pre-empt the individual's right to choose. Critics also point out that although there have been many studies of the effect of fluoridation on cavities, there have been few studies that look at overall health effects. Fluoride is toxic in large quantities when it can interfere with calcium absorption, leading to bone disorders and heart disease. Although the levels in drinking water are relatively small, fluoride does accumulate in the body, and it may be linked to cancer. It may also increase the amount of aluminium that will dissolve into the water, which may be linked to dementia (see 'Major Contaminants').

Proponents maintain that fluoridated water is safe. The World Health Organisation has reviewed the epidemiological studies and concluded that there is no evidence that fluoride causes cancer in humans. You must make up your own mind.

The Bottom Line

We have come a long way since the days of widespread cholera and typhoid caused by contaminated water supplies, but the fact remains that water treatment is not perfect. Standard processes improve water quality, but they do not remove all the industrial and agricultural contaminants that make their way into water supplies. Many of these are new or recently discovered. The combined effects of most of them are unknown. Some of them can be removed by advanced (and expensive) processes, some cannot.

The best (and cheapest) option is to prevent chemical contaminants from getting into the water system in the first place, by enacting and enforcing strict source control regulations. This would mean that industries would be required to remove contaminants from their effluent before they discharged it, instead of leaving the contaminants for water treatment plants to deal with. By the time water reaches the treatment plants, it can contain a cocktail of unknown substances from thousands of sources. It is far easier to remove contaminants at source, where it may even be possible to recycle them. But so long as it's cheaper for industries to dump their effluent into water courses, and so long as regulations are not strict or strictly enforced, dumping will be their preferred option.

Water treatment can also add undesirable substances into drinking water, such as chlorine by-products and aluminium. Finally, contamination can occur after treatment, such as when polyaromatic hydrocarbons leach out of mains lined with coal tar pitch, or when domestic pipes are lead (see 'Major Contaminants').

More optimistically, regulations are constantly getting stricter and the public is becoming more aware of water quality issues.

Chapter Four

Where does it go?

The Distribution System

Modern water treatment and distribution is a massive engineering feat. Thousands of kilometres of pipes carry water from distant sources to centralised treatment plants where it is cleaned, and then to individual homes, where clean water flows out of taps on demand.

First, raw water has to get from the source (either groundwater or surface water or both) to the treatment plant. Usually the plants are located close to the source, but this is not always the case. Water is transferred to the treatment plants through pipes or open channels.

Once it has been treated, water must be delivered to consumers. This is done through the distribution system — an underground maze of pipes and tanks. There is no 'national grid' for water like there is for electricity — each region has its own separate system of pipes and tanks. However, some water travels very long distances. For example, drinking water in Birmingham is piped from Wales (see the map, opposite). Rivers themselves are often used as conduits for transporting water from one region to another. In some areas, particularly the south east, water is recycled several times in its journey from source to sea. In view of recent shortages, plans exist for extended grids.

After treatment, water is usually stored in service reservoirs. Reservoirs serve two functions: they store enough water to meet

—————————Long distance water movements—————————

Use this map to see very generally where water is transported across the
country. Due to local detail it is impossible to show on a map of this scale the
definite origin of your specific tapwater, only general movements. Information
from Scotland and Northern Ireland was not available at time of publication.

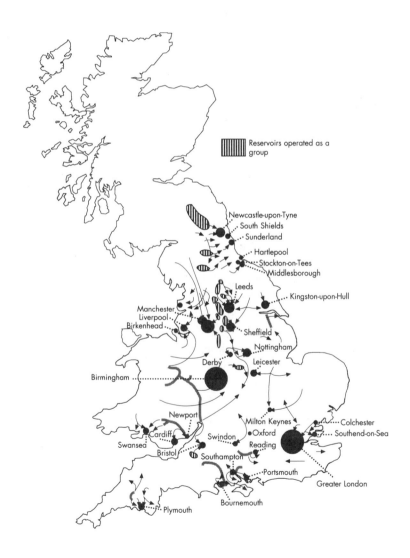

Where is treated water used?

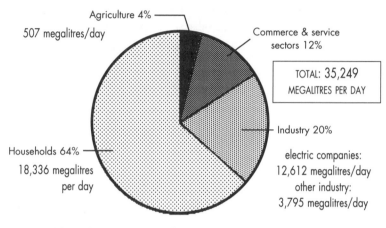

Agriculture 4%
507 megalitres/day

Commerce & service
sectors 12%

TOTAL: 35,249
MEGALITRES PER DAY

Industry 20%

electric companies:
12,612 megalitres/day
other industry:
3,795 megalitres/day

Households 64%
18,336 megalitres
per day

Households are the biggest users of treated water.

peak demand, and, if in a raised position, they create water pressure in the mains. Sometimes water towers are used to create pressure in very flat areas. From the reservoir, the water travels through a network of trunk mains, which take water from service reservoirs and supply it to feeder mains. The principal feeder mains take the water from trunk mains and deliver it to focal points within the distribution network. Finally, there is a network of small mains that distribute water from the feeder mains to consumers' supply pipes. This is where the distribution system ends and, with it, the water supplier's responsibilities.

There are pumps and valves located within the distribution system: booster pumps are used to ensure sufficient flow rates and sufficient pressure; strategic valves allow parts of the system to be isolated for repairs. The connection between the small mains and the consumer supply pipes is stopcocked within the boundary of the dwelling.

End Uses

Household water use accounts for 64% of all water use, and 40% of all abstractions; that is, 160 litres per day for every man, woman and child, or a staggering 380 litres per household per day. A third of this is used for flushing toilets — see 'Reducing Water

———————— Toxic algae in reservoirs ————————

During the hot, dry summer of 1989, blooms of toxic blue-green algae contaminated more than 50 bodies of water, including reservoirs. The algae hit the headlines when people who swam in the reservoirs developed skin allergies, cold-like symptoms, asthma and stomach disorders and several dogs and sheep died from drinking the water. In other countries, algal toxins in drinking water have caused serious cases of gastroenteritis. The Drinking Water Inspectorate commissioned a four-year study into the situation. It concluded the level of algal toxins in tap water was not a health hazard to consumers drinking it, but swimming in reservoirs contaminated with the algae could be dangerous.

Consumption'. One fifth goes to industry, 12% to the commerce and service sectors, and 4% to agriculture (see diagram opposite). Not all abstracted water is treated: some applications such as agriculture and electricity generation can use raw, untreated water.

Is there enough?
Water Demand

Water demand depends on the population of an area and the amount each person in that area consumes (the 'per capita consumption'). Predicting future demand is difficult: it must take into account changes in birth rate, movement of people in and out of the area in question, changes in consumption per person, and industrial demand (which is highly dependent on economic factors). In the past, predictions have tended to overestimate the increase in consumption per person.

Having said that, UK water consumption has grown, on average, one percent a year since 1961 and it is probable it will continue to rise. The National Rivers Authority, in 1992, expected an increase of 13.5% by the year 2011. However in 1995 Ofwat (the consumer watchdog) said it didn't expect demand to grow a great deal until 2014 -15. Much of the increased demand in the past has been for piped mains water, an increase of 13% from 1980 to 1989. Domestic consumption was expected to keep rising as more households acquired water-using equipment, such as washing machines and dishwashers. Yet since 1992 consumption has fallen, in all sectors, but this may be a temporary trend.

——————————*What makes a drought?*——————————

It doesn't take a big change in rainfall patterns to cause a drought. Most of the water supply for the summer and autumn is collected in the winter, when much less water is lost through evaporation and transpiration. A drop of 20% in winter rainfall can mean the reservoirs don't fill up, and that almost certainly leads to water restrictions in the summer. Of course, any time there is a prolonged dry period, there is a risk of drought, especially if surface water is the main source of drinking water, but dry winters are particularly dangerous.

Industrial demand has declined overall, partly due to economic recessions, but partly to more efficient use of water by industries and the fact that most new (service) industries do not consume large quantities of water. Demand is not expected to rise substantially in the next few decades. Agricultural use has increased dramatically in the past twenty years, but this still represents only a tiny fraction of total demand. Leaks account for 25-29% of all treated water (see page 57).

Some regions have plenty of water resources to meet demand, others do not (see graph, opposite). The demand is expected to rise most quickly in south and south east England, where there is also the lowest annual rainfall, the greatest use of available water resources, and many rivers with unacceptably low flows.

In dry weather, there is more demand for water in the Thames region than there is water. This demand is met by reusing water (see later).

Water Supplies

The law requires water suppliers to provide consumers with adequate quantities of water. However, this does not mean unlimited amounts of water. According to the Department of the Environment, "the statutory duty on water companies to provide customers with a sufficient supply of water has never been interpreted as an obligation to provide unrestricted supplies of water at all times". Furthermore, water suppliers are not required to provide water for outdoor needs, such as washing cars or watering lawns. Section 52 of the 1991 Water Industry Act only requires that

Up against the limit?

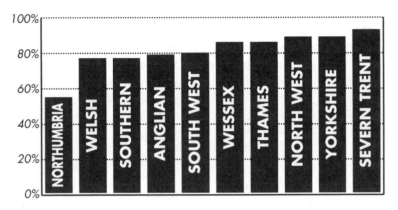

The graph shows the amount of public water being used, compared to how much there is, in each region of England and Wales in 1993-94. In Scotland, despite higher rainfall, shortages are also being experienced. Since the 1995-96 drought the situation has worsened, due to rainfall being 75% of normal, on average. Therefore hosepipe bans and regular drought orders are to become the norm until the situation is rectified. *Source: Dept. of Environment.*

homes be supplied with water for domestic purposes: drinking, washing, cooking, central heating and flushing toilets.

Ofwat defines a reasonable level of water availability as follows: hosepipe bans should occur, on average, not more than once in ten years, major publicity campaigns for voluntary reduction not more than once in twenty years, and rota cuts or standpipes not more than once in one hundred years.

However, defining adequate supplies using long-term averages makes it difficult to judge whether water suppliers are currently fulfilling their obligations. In 1992-95 42% of the population was subject to voluntary reductions and 13% was subject to formal hosepipe bans. There have been four major dry periods in the past twenty years: 1971-76, 1984, 1988-92, and 1995-96 (see box on page 56). This may just be a statistical blip, but it may signal long-term climate changes, an eventuality it is prudent to assume. If it's the case that our weather is changing, the Ofwat guidelines can't be achieved with current water management strategies.

────Drought orders, England and Wales────

1976	136 drought orders	1987	0
1977	0	1988	0
1978	19	1989	89
1979	0	1990	61
1980	4	1991	28
1981	0	1992	16
1982	15	1993	0
1983	6	1994	0
1984	104	1995	53
1985	0	1996	30 (by May)
1986	0		

These figures are for both ordinary and emergency drought orders. As of May 1996, there are three means of dealing with droughts: ordinary drought orders, emergency ones and drought permits. A pre-requisite for them all is exceptional shortage of rain entailing a serious deficiency of supplies. All of these measures can authorise abstraction from unspecified sources and can modify or suspend restrictions or obligations. Drought orders and drought permits can last up to six months, with extensions up to one year. Emergency drought orders may be granted where the deficiency may "impair the economic or social well-being of persons in the affected area". They give the water company complete discretion on the uses of water, and last up to three months, but may be extended to five. The new drought permits give more limited powers and are granted by the Environment Agency and navigation authorities, the others by the Secretary of State.

In 1995 there were five emergency drought orders, entailing restrictions such as car wash bans. Interestingly, although there were standpipes in Yorkshire, these were not authorised by an emergency drought order and appear to have been a speculative, opinion-testing move by Yorkshire Water.

Up against the limit?

Are we running out of water? This may seem an absurd question, but one which arises as a question of management; put another way, it means: are we managing our water resources effectively? In 1995, 34,000,000 cubic metres of water per day were abstracted in England and Wales; approximately the equivalent of about 700 litres per person per day. Approximately 20% of abstractions are from groundwater, although this varies considerably from region to region. If the amount of water abstracted exceeds the amount of rainfall recharging water sources, the natural water table will be lowered and river flow will be reduced. This is not good news, either for the quality and quantity of our drinking water, or for the aquatic environment. As the water table drops, wells dry up, there is less river flow to dilute sewage and industrial effluents. Frogs, fish and other aquatic life have less water to live in (and what they have is more polluted); it also affects the recreational aspects of the rivers.

The National Rivers Authority had, and the Environment Agency now has, responsibility for dealing with this. Since 1990/91 the NRA estimated that it had reduced low flow from 335km to 207km along the forty rivers it reckoned are under the highest risk in England and Wales. The target is to reduce it to 79km by 1996-97. It is unclear how this is going to be achieved with current low rainfall patterns, however. In January 1996, average river flows in the major rivers of England and Wales were under 50% of the January average. The worst rivers were the Nene in East Anglia (9%), and the Ribble and Lune in Lancashire (both as low as 8%). Several of the recent and current drought orders are for releases from reservoirs to compensate for low flow in rivers.

Groundwater abstraction can cause a special problem in coastal waters. If too much groundwater is taken from aquifers near coastal areas, salt water will flow into the aquifer and contaminate it — a process called 'saline intrusion'. Saline intrusion is difficult and very expensive to reverse. Currently it is a problem in aquifers near the Mersey, Humber and Thames estuaries.

Larger Scale Reuse

There are various ways to re-use water on a larger scale. Indirect re-use involves discharging water that has already been used for domestic or industrial purposes into fresh surface or underground waters, where it is diluted and then subsequently

——————*Water recycling in the South East*——————

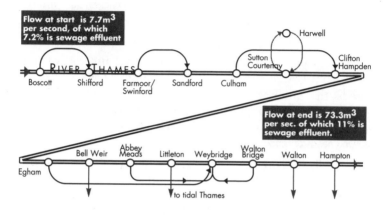

Flow at start is 7.7m³ per second, of which 7.2% is sewage effluent

Harwell

RIVER THAMES

Boscott   Shifford   Farmoor/   Sandford   Culham   Sutton   Clifton
                     Swinford   Courtenay   Hampden

Flow at end is 73.3m³ per sec. of which 11% is sewage effluent.

Egham   Bell Weir   Abbey   Littleton   Weybridge   Walton   Walton   Hampton
                    Meads   Bridge

to tidal Thames

Adapted from Dean and Lund (1981), pub. Academic Press Ltd.

Supplying London with drinking water is not an easy task. The city has a population of more than 10 million people and it's located in the part of the country with the smallest volume of water resources. London's water comes from three main sources: boreholes, the Thames itself, and tributaries of the Thames, which include in their volume a staggering 1.2 million cubic metres of treated sewage a day. People living along the River Thames are drinking water, some of which has been drunk several times already, as the above schematic map shows (the figures represent average flows). Walton Bridge, in the Thames area, actually discharges its effluent upstream of its intake. For this reason, water taken from the rivers is stored for seven days before treatment — sand filtration<$Ifiltration;sand and then chlorination. Sewage is treated to a very high standard before it is discharged, and ammonia and nitrates are completely removed.

On average, the recycle rate is only 13% but it can vary dramatically according to rainfall and river flow patterns; it has exceeded 100% in the past. So the Thames contains large volumes of wastewater — on a dry summer's day, its flow can be as much as 95% effluent. When water is recycled many times, dissolved salts can accumulate, giving the water an unpleasant taste and causing scaling and corrosion in pipes. There are also suspected health risks, such as low male sperm counts.

The new ring main around London, a major feat of modern engineering, helps to transport water to where it is needed.

The River Darent

The Darent is among the 40 rivers identified by the National Rivers Authority as having a dangerously low flow. It runs south east of London and eventually flows into the Thames.

Beginning in 1945, boreholes were drilled into the Darent valley to supply water for south east London — by the 1950s, local residents were complaining their private wells were drying up. Over the years, the water table continued to drop, as more and more boreholes sucked up the groundwater to supply the growing needs of London.

In 1985, the Thames Water Authority built a trunk sewer that ran along the river to the point where it joined the Thames. The idea was to discharge sewage where there was greater flow to dilute it. Unfortunately, this meant that although water was being taken out of the Darent, it wasn't being returned. The result has been that the final one to two miles of the river dry up on a regular basis.

---

used as a source of water. This is quite common — anyone living on the lower stretches of a river is probably drinking water that contains treated wastewater from towns and cities upstream.

Direct re-use is when treated wastewater is deliberately re-used for another purpose, such as irrigation, recreation, industry, recharging underground aquifers, or drinking. Finally, there is in-plant water recycling, the re-use of water within industrial plants. Many industries, such as paper mills, currently re-use much of their water because it is cheaper to recycle it than to pay the fees for discharging polluted water.

The key to re-use is to treat wastewater adequately for its intended purpose. For example, it is not necessary to remove nitrate and phosphate from municipal wastewater if it is to be used for irrigation — plants thrive on these nutrients. However, they may be a problem if the wastewater is to be used for industrial processes.

After primary treatment (screening, grit removal and sediment-ation), wastewater can be used for irrigating orchards. After secondary treatment (clarification), it can be used for agricultural and landscape irrigation, as well as certain types of groundwater recharge. After tertiary treatment (nitrogen removal, lime treatment, and filtration), it can be used for industrial processes and cooling water, groundwater recharge by injection, non-contact recreation, and aquaculture.

Thirty per cent of all our drinking water is recycled, on average. In the south east this can rise dramatically (see the box on page 58). In dry seasons the Thames and Lee can even be 95% treated effluent. Even though treatment standards may be high, there may well be health risks associated with this. Several studies have found that there may be long-term effects of reusing water for drinking. There are higher rates of cancer in people whose drinking water supply comes from river water containing treated wastewater than in people who drink groundwater. A recent study even suggested that the quality of London's water could be a factor in declining male fertility. When water is recycled many times dissolved salts — such as nitrates, chlorides, phosphates and sulphates — build up in it. These may increase toxicity, bad tastes, and encourage deterioration of the pipes. These salts are persistent but can be removed by expensive techniques such as reverse osmosis and ion exchange. Naturally this has implications for the cost to the consumer.

What is to be done to meet demand?

In the past, water suppliers met increased demand by sinking new boreholes and opening up new reservoirs. But this is expensive and environmentally damaging. Another possibility for alleviating the supply and low flow problems is to bring in more water from areas of high rainfall to areas of low rainfall. The National Rivers Authority, together with the relevant water service companies, have come up with a number of possible schemes for doing this. These include transferring water from the Severn (which comes from mid-Wales) to both the Thames and the Trent via canals; redirecting some water from the Vyrnwy reservoir to the Severn; enlarging the mid-Wales Craig Goch reservoir and feeding water from there to the Severn and Thames; feeding water from the Trent to East Anglia; new, or enlarged, reservoirs in south west Oxfordshire and East Anglia; and tapping into Birmingham's rising groundwater; Yorkshire Water plans to use the Kielder reservoir surplus for meeting deficits in Yorkshire. However it takes up to twenty years to implement a major engineering scheme of this kind, and it remains to be seen which options will be taken up. Estuary dams for fresh water have been ruled out for the present.

As the cost of providing acceptable drinking water goes up and as new water resources become increasingly scarce, reducing demand is becoming the preferred option. The Government's current position is that existing resources should be used to the fullest possible extent. The water industry claims it is examining opportunities for water conservation and demand management. But can we believe them?

Wastage in the Pipes

Before large engineering works are carried out it would make sense to make a better use of the water we have gathered. This makes economic and environmental sense: reducing water consumption is a cheap, effective way to make best use of the finite water resources available. Estimates of the water in the mains that never reaches the end user vary from almost a quarter to 29%. Some of this water is drawn off for fire fighting, flushing water mains or sewers, and street cleaning, but the majority is leakage from service reservoirs, the mains themselves, and customers' pipes.

Water leakage is greatest when the water is acidic, where the terrain is hilly (necessitating high pressures), or where there are long distances between customers.

3,750 million litres a day leak from the supply pipes in England and Wales. This is almost one fifth of all the water collected and processed (18%) — enough to satisfy the domestic needs of about half the population. Yorkshire Water, whose customers have suffered the most from the drought of 1995-96, is leaking enough water to satisfy the demands of 8 million people. These are according to the water companies' own figures. On page 60 are the figures for leakage for the ten privatised water companies, showing which companies are the leakiest.

Do customers waste more water through leaks than the

Who leaks the most?

Company	Total daily pipe leakage (millions of litres)	Millions of people in the company area whose daily needs this would serve.
North West	718.6	5.5
Thames	627.2	4
Severn Trent	523.8	4
Yorkshire	472.7	3.7
Welsh	295.4	2
Anglian	152.7	1
Wessex	117.6	0.9
South West	115	0.8
Southern	87.5	0.6
Northumbrian	71.8	0.5

companies? No. They do manage to lose 1,000 million litres a day but the companies leak three and a half times more. This means that companies are better off cutting leaks in their own pipes and encouraging customers to cut their own leaks than they are encouraging people to install water meters. In fact the NRA recommended that cutting leaks is more than twice as useful as installing meters. The water companies at present have no set of targets for cutting leaks, and have not said how much they are prepared to spend on cutting leaks. The NRA has admonished Ofwat for not forcing the water companies to reduce their own leaks by setting mandatory levels. According to the Water Services Association — the companies' spokesbody — it is not<$Icost;equipment economic to replace mains unless there are four or more leaks or bursts per kilometre each year. Clearly there is not enough effective regulation on this issue.

For more on this topic, turn to the sections on privatisation and water conservation.

Chapter Five

How is it managed?

Regulating Water

The regulation of drinking water is a complex area, governed by several levels of legislation and enforced by different bodies. This makes it difficult if you have a problem. The major regulations are described below.

EC Regulations

There are several EC directives regarding water, including the following:

• the quality of surface water for abstraction for drinking water (75/440/EEC),

• the protection of groundwater (80/68/EEC),

• the regulation of discharge of dangerous substances into the aquatic environment (76/464/EEC) (plus sub-directives for each specific substance), and

• the quality of water intended for human consumption (80/778/EEC).

This last one, 80/778/EC (commonly known as the EC drinking water directive), sets standards for 46 parameters. These 'maximum admissible concentrations' are incorporated in the UK Water Regulations described below. Some of the parameters are currently under revision.

————————————*Court actions*————————————

On 27th March 1995, Welsh Water became the first supplier to be convicted of breaching drinking water regulations. It was charged for not taking proper precautions when relining water mains in Anglesey in 1993. The incident occurred when a Welsh Water subsidiary was spraying epoxy resins on the internal surface of water mains to protect them against corrosion. According to the regulations, the water supplier should have looked at videos of the pipe interior to make sure the epoxy had set properly before the mains were put back in use. However, the videos were never taken. There was no evidence drinking water quality had been affected, but the supplier was fined £1000.

The following month, Severn Trent Water was convicted of supplying water 'unfit for human consumption' by allowing contaminated water to flow into the mains. In 1994 a solvent recycling plant in Shropshire illegally discharged solvents that made their way downstream and into a Worcester water treatment plant. Staff at the treatment plant failed to detect the contamination until they received complaints from consumers that their tap water tasted and smelled repellent. Over 140,000 consumers were affected. The Court ruled that the company was at fault because it had not tested the water as frequently as the guidelines called for. Although the solvent was not a threat to human health, and although Severn Trent notified consumers promptly when it discovered the problem and brought in replacement water by tanker, the Court found the supplier guilty.

UK Regulations

The UK Water Regulations are an improvement on EC standards because they incorporate all the EC standards, plus standards for an additional eleven parameters. The key parameters are coliforms, nitrate, aluminium, lead, trihalomethanes, polycyclicaromatic hydrocarbons, and pesticides. The regulations define how each parameter is to be measured and how frequently samples are to be taken. Legal action can be taken against water suppliers who do not meet these standards (see box above). The 1989 Water Supply (Water Quality) Regulations are now consolidated in the 1991 Water Industry Act.

The EC Drinking Water Directive allows the UK to grant 'relaxations' or 'derogations' — special permits allowing water companies not to conform with particular standards over a specific period of time. Derogations are only permitted for non-toxic substances and characteristics, such as colour, sulphates, magnesium, sodium and potassium, and only under certain circumstances — for example, where the local geology or weather conditions make it extremely hard to meet standards. About three percent of the UK population drinks water that has been granted derogations, at any one time.

When the water industry was privatised, the UK government also accepted 'undertakings' from many water suppliers, allowing them to delay meeting EC standards. This was not legal according to EC regulations, but they were granted for limited periods of time to give suppliers a chance to upgrade their treatment facilities. Critics consider that these undertakings are a legal loophole that enable water suppliers to ignore EC standards.

Administration
England and Wales

Until recently, there was a multitude of bodies responsible for enforcing different aspects of the Water Industry Act: the Drinking Water Inspectorate, the National Rivers Authority, Her Majesty's Inspectorate of Pollution, the Office of Water Services (Ofwat) and local authorities. Some of these have been merged — on April 1 1996 the Environment Bill came into effect, merging the NRA, HMIP and the waste regulatory authorities into one body, the Environment Agency. The Drinking Water Inspectorate, Ofwat, and local authorities remain unaffected.

Under the Water Industry Act, the Secretary of State (for the Environment or Wales) is empowered to force the water companies to comply with their duties to keep water quality high, if they are failing. *The Drinking Water Inspectorate* (DWI) helps the relevant Secretary to protect public health.

Its duties are: to ensure that water suppliers comply with their statutory duties; to carry out annual assessments of water samples from treatment works, service reservoirs, and water supply zones; to inspect individual companies; to check data provided by the companies; to provide technical and scientific advice to the

——————Company regions in England & Wales——————

Department of the Environment and Welsh Office; to assess and respond to consumer complaints when local procedures have been exhausted; to identify and assess new issues or hazards relating to drinking water quality and initiate research as required; and to give authoritative guidance on analytical methods used to monitor drinking water.

The DWI has been slow to recommend prosecution of water suppliers that breach regulations; between 1989 and 1995, there were no prosecutions and critics complain that the Inspectorate is not effectively enforcing drinking water regulations. In part, this is due to understaffing — the DWI does not have enough inspectors thoroughly to audit suppliers, and so they rely heavily on

Water suppliers in England & Wales

Each region has sewage treatment serviced by a single company, but there may be several water supply companies.

Anglia Region
Anglian Water Services Ltd
Cambridge Water Company
East Anglian Water Company
Essex Water Company
Tendring Hundred Water Company

Northumbria Region
Northumbrian Water Ltd
Hartlepool's Water Company
Newcastle and Gateshead Water Company
Sunderland and South Shields Water Company

North West Region
North West Water Ltd

Severn Trent Region
Severn Trent Water Ltd
East Worcestershire Waterworks Company
South Staffordshire Waterworks Company

Southern Region
Southern Water Services Ltd
Eastbourne Water Company
Folkestone and District Water Company
Mid-Kent Water Company
Mid-Sussex Water Company
Portsmouth Water plc

West Kent Water Company

South West Region
South West Water Services Ltd

Thames Region
Thames Water Utilities Ltd
Colne Valley Water plc
East Surrey Water plc
Lee Valley Water plc
Mid-Southern Water Company
North Surrey Water Company
Rickmansworth Water plc
Sutton District Water plc

Wales Region
Dwr Cymru (Welsh Water)
Chester Waterworks Company
Wrexham and East Denbighshire Water Company

Wessex Region
Wessex Water Services Ltd
Bournemouth and District Water Company
Bristol Waterworks Company
West Hampshire Water Company

Yorkshire Region
Yorkshire Water Services Ltd
York Waterworks plc

——Who regulates the water supply companies?——

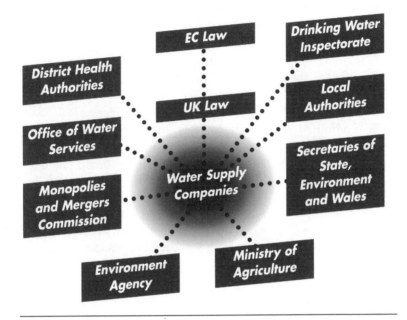

suppliers monitoring themselves. However, in 1995 the DWI recommended the prosecution of two suppliers, who were subsequently convicted of breaching regulations (see box on page 64).

The Office of Water Services (Ofwat) is the water industry watchdog. It protects consumers against abuse by a monopoly. It is independent of the companies but linked to the Department of Trade and Industry. Its job is to regulate the level of services provided by water suppliers and the charges they make to customers.

The Director General of Ofwat is also responsible for the ten local Customer Service Committees (see the Resource Guide and next chapter) which are supposed to represent consumers' views and investigate complaints.

The Environment Agency is responsible for providing high quality, integrated environmental protection, management and enhancement of land, water and air. It takes over the responsibilities of the old National Rivers Authority (NRA), which include water resource management; authorising and controlling abstractions, and augmenting river flows to support abstraction; pollution control in inland waters, estuarial waters and coastal waters; flood defence; land drainage; salmon and freshwater fisheries; nature conservation; and recreation. It also takes over the responsibilities of Her Majesty's Inspectorate of Pollution (HMIP), which enforced the regulations controlling dangerous substances and industrial effluent. Like the DWI, there were doubts about HMIP's effectiveness at policing industrial discharges. HMIP had publicly admitted there were too few staff to deal with all the complaints it received. How the Environment Agency will perform is anyone's guess at the moment, but hopefully its broad mandate means it will take a more integrated approach to water quality issues.

Local authorities are responsible for monitoring the quality and sufficiency of public water supplies, for monitoring private water supplies and for enforcing public health requirements.

Scotland

Scotland is covered under the 1990 Water (Scotland) Act. Water and sewerage services were provided by the Regional and Islands Councils, but on 1 April 1996, three new Water Authorities were established for the west, east and north. These are public, rather than private, bodies since the Scottish Office received overwhelming lobbies against privatisation in 1995. At the same time, the Scottish Environment Protection Agency was established, amalgamating the old River Purification Boards, the River Purification Authority functions of the Islands Council, and Her Majesty's Industrial Pollution Inspectorate. The Agency is responsible for discharge consents, water conservation, abstraction licenses, and pollution monitoring. The agency is divided into West, East and North regions, in correspondence with the areas covered by the Water Authorities.

Northern Ireland

In Northern Ireland, water resources, water conservation, water supplies, sewerage services and water pollution control are all handled by the Department of the Environment.

Privatisation in England and Wales

The water industry in England and Wales was privatised in 1989, creating ten water service companies, which provide water and sewerage services, and 29 water-only companies. This was a very controversial move and many people opposed it.

There are several basic arguments against privatisation. Firstly, the primary duty of a privatised company is to its shareholders, not to its customers. It must create profits, but the water business is a low growth area, and there is little money to be made in conserving water or improving its quality. Furthermore, because the private water suppliers are granted regional monopolies, consumers can hardly shop around for better water or better service if they are unhappy. Finally, privatised companies must be policed to ensure they meet their obligations. The question is, are they policed strictly enough?

The graph on the next page shows how capital investment by the water companies compares with profits, dividends to shareholders — and costs to customers.

In the six years since privatisation, results have been mixed. While water prices have increased dramatically and company directors reap huge salaries, many parts of the country have been hit with drought orders and hosepipe bans (see 'Supply and Demand'). The main beneficiary of salary increases has been the Chief Executive of Thames Water, whose salary has increased by 806% since privatisation. At the time of writing this post is filled by Mike Hoffman, who is, incidentally, also the President of the Water Services Association, the umbrella group for nine of the ten privatised water companies. (Wessex Water recently resigned from the WSA.) Such salary rises are defended as being in line with similar salaries in the private sector. However, they need also to be justified by improved performance.

Privatised companies have been able to put an influx of much-needed capital into the sewage and water systems. This was particularly necessary to meet the stricter EC standards. Between 1989 and 1995, water suppliers poured £15 billion into water and sewage capital works. However, most of this was in the earlier years, and investment has since tailed off. There has, it is true, been a significant improvement in complying with drinking water

Privatisation — the winners and loser

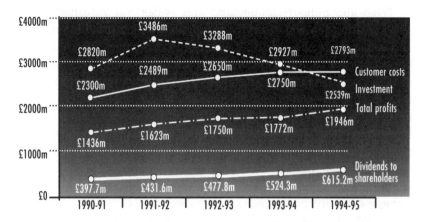

The figures speak for themselves. Since privatisation in 1990, capital investment in new plant and distribution by the 10 water companies in England and Wales has gone down by £282 million (10%), while dividends have risen by £217.5 million (55%), profits by £510 million (36%), total boardroom salaries have shot up from £540,000 to £2.4 million (444%) and the total annual cost of providing water to you, the customers, has risen by £294 million (12%).
Source: Annual Reports and the Labour Party.

standards, fewer homes at risk from low water pressure or sewer flooding, and an improvement in the quality of sewage effluent, rivers and beaches, as reported in the 1996 Department of the Environment publication, *Indicators of Sustainable Development for the UK*.

However, on the question of unplanned disconnections or interruptions to supply, in 1993-5 there were 183,852 occasions when this occurred without warning. The worst offender has been Yorkshire Water, with a figure of 69,513. Further, the number of complaints to the companies has also risen from 11.3 million a year in 1990-91 to a staggering 15.4 million a year in 1995. This could mean that people feel it is easier to complain than it was before privatisation — but it still reveals a large body of discontent. The sheer number of complaints should warn the companies not to be complacent.

What about the disconnection of customers who do not pay their bills? Many groups, including the British Medical Association and the National Consumer Council, have argued that because water is a basic necessity, it should not be legal to cut off someone's supply, and that water suppliers should be restricted to collecting bad debts through the courts. As yet there is no legislation to prohibit suppliers from disconnecting customers, but official figures show that disconnections have decreased significantly since privatisation.

The official figures are misleading, however, because many disconnections are not recorded in the official figures. This is because of the introduction of pre-payment devices for low-income customers, an extremely controversial step which is examined in the next section.

With the prospect of drought orders being a regular feature every summer, and of consumer prices rising while capital investment is falling and boardroom pay and dividends are rising, it is not surprising that the water service companies are the subject of intense interest and criticism. The Labour Party does not plan to re-nationalise the industry if re-elected, but it does say it plans to introduce more effective controls.

The root of the problems to do with privatisation is that the old water authorities had a statutory responsibility to supply water to customers; the water companies, in addition, have a responsibility to shareholders. This compromises the quality of their service when measured against the cost to the consumer. Perhaps this is the reason why a 1995 poll in Scotland found 97% against privatisation of the industry there.

Paying For Water

Water may be free when it falls from the sky, but collecting, treating and distributing it costs money. The biggest expense in providing drinking water is treatment, particularly if it involves sedimentation and filtration (see 'Water Treatment Plants'). The poorer the quality of the raw water, the more expensive the treatment process will be.

How much does it cost?

Where is it cheaper to take a bath?

Thames Water	10p
Severn Trent	11p
Northumbrian	12p
North West	12p
Yorkshire	12p
Southern	14p
Wessex	14p
Dŵr Cymru	15p
Anglian	16p
South West	18p

1996 costs based on an 80 litre bath.

How much does it cost to...?

Take a shower	6p
Use the dishwasher	6p
Flush the toilet	2p
Use the washing machine	12p
Use the garden sprinkler (1hr)	80p
Leave tap dripping (per day)[1]	15p
Leave tap running while cleaning your teeth (per minute)[2]	2p

[1] — assumes 90 litres per day.

[2] — assumes 9 litres per minute.

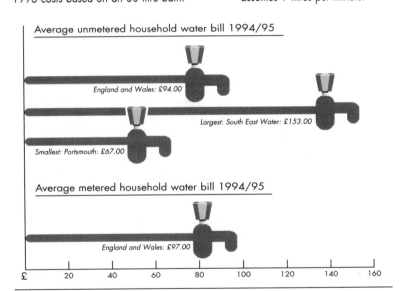

Average unmetered household water bill 1994/95

England and Wales: £94.00

Largest: South East Water: £153.00

Smallest: Portsmouth: £67.00

Average metered household water bill 1994/95

England and Wales: £97.00

£ 20 40 60 80 100 120 140 160

England and Wales

Like other privatised utility industries, increases in the price of water for domestic consumers are calculated by a formula enforced by a regulator, in this case Ofwat. Unlike other privatised utilities, water prices are allowed to rise significantly to fund improvements in water quality. Thus, from 1990/91 to 1994/95, the average unmetered water and sewerage combined bill rose by 77%, and in some areas the increase was as much as 150%. It is worth noting that even with these dramatic increases, water prices in the UK are comparable with prices in other European countries. However, before privatisation of the industry, average domestic prices rose from £86 in 1985-86 to £134 in 1990-91, a rise of 56%.

Water suppliers set the price of water according to a complicated formula set by Ofwat. The formula is based on the retail price index, which reflects inflation rates, and the 'K' factor — a figure established annually by Ofwat that reflects the need to finance major improvements in water treatment.

Are we paying too much? Many people think so. Since privatisation, 67,402,212 queries about bills had been received by the beginning of 1996, and the number of queries has increased every year since 1990.

Most domestic households pay unmetered water charges based on the rateable value of property; most businesses pay metered charges.

Scotland

Currently domestic water bills are based on council tax bands and collected through the personal community water charge; industry is charged a non-domestic water rate. Metering became an option for all users under the 1992 Local Government Finance Act, but there are hardly any installed domestic meters.

Northern Ireland

Domestic consumers' water bills are based mainly on the rateable value of property. Metering is not available for domestic customers, and there is no consumer council or regulator.

The Water Metering Debate

Since most consumers in England and Wales pay a flat rate for water, there is no financial incentive to reduce the amount of water they use. Even if the tap runs all day long, the water bill at the end of the month doesn't change.

The Department of the Environment believes the solution to excessive water consumption is water metering. According to a

——Methods of charging for water 1994/95——

- in England and Wales

5.5% of **households** pay <u>metered</u> water charges

94.5% of **households** pay <u>unmetered</u> water charges
usually based on rateable value of property.

73% of **business** customers pay <u>metered</u> water charges

27% of **business** customers pay <u>unmetered</u> water charges

1992 consultation paper, *Using Water Wisely*: "If customers pay for water by volume, they are in a position to decide how much they want to spend on water. They have an incentive to economise in their use of water by cutting out waste, and to spend money for that purpose up to the point where the cost of further water-saving measures exceeds the amount they would save in water charges."

In 1988, in conjunction with the water companies, the Department of the Environment funded national trials to determine how big an impact metering would have on water consumption over a period of five years. Twelve areas were selected as trial sites: Hutton Rudby, South Normanton, Bromsgrove, Brookmans Park, Chorleywood, Bristol, Camberley, Croydon, Chandlers Ford, Poole, and the Isle of Wight. The results were an average reduction in demand by 13% and a reduction in peak demand by as much as 30%. Fifty-nine percent of customers involved in the trials said they had taken steps to reduce water consumption.

Since then, the level of domestic metering has increased from less than 1% of households in 1989 to 7% in 1995. So far, only Anglian Water has made metering compulsory. All water companies will provide customers with meters on request, but Ofwat reports that many of the metering options offered are inflexible and costly.

How would metering affect you? The cost of installing a meter is £200 to £300 per household, which you would pay. Thus far, the Government has not guaranteed financial aid to metered customers on low incomes or to those with exceptional water needs. If you use lots of water and live in a low rateable value property, metering would almost certainly be more expensive. If you use relatively little water and have a high rateable value property, metering might reduce your water bill. So in the end, you would probably pay more for metered water to cover the additional costs of a metered supply.

According to the 1991 Strategy of the Director General of Water Services, water metering is the best conservation solution for most properties in the longer term. However, given the cost of a rapid switch to universal metering, it does not advocate metering all properties in the short term.

Many groups are opposed to widespread domestic metering. Welsh Water argues that most of its costs as a water supplier are fixed, not tied to volume. The Consumers' Association is concerned that the capital costs of installing meters and the ongoing costs of maintaining, calibrating and reading meters would result in further, unnecessary increases in the cost of water for all customers.

There are also practical difficulties in metering all domestic dwellings: many houses share joint service pipes, a row of houses is often fed by a common service pipe at the rear, blocks of flats have one common supply pipe, and sometimes meters cannot be put inside a house without causing significant disruption to fixtures. So there is considerable debate on whether the water saved by metering outweighs the costs.

Ultimately, the question is whether metering is the most effective way to reduce water consumption. A 1993 report by the Parliamentary Office of Science and Technology concluded that because leakage in water company pipes accounted for a 22% loss of water supply, leakage control would be better value for money than a universal metering programme.

But if not water metering, then what? The UK Government has indicated that water suppliers in England and Wales should not continue to use rateable property value as a basis for charges. That leaves either a flat rate charge or some kind of banding system, possibly based on council tax data. There is no clear consensus on which way to go. Whatever method is chosen, there will inevitably be losers, but any solution should not be used as an excuse or smokescreen to raise charges and profits, but as a cost-effective solution to water supply and quality problems.

Pre-payment devices

Sometimes known as 'Waterkeys', these devices have been called a back door way of raising charges, while making life easier for the water companies. Recently, we have seen the introduction of these devices by all three of the formerly nationalised utilities (gas and electricity too). They are intended to help low-income households with their bills. They involve purchasing credit on an electronic card, usually for £5 each time, from the post office. The cards are then inserted into a 'meter', called a 'device' to distinguish them from water meters. In the case of water, £5 credit buys you a week's supply — *regardless of how much water you use.*

If the card is not recharged, a valve automatically shuts off the water supply, after an emergency supply period.

Consumer groups do not like these devices. They argue that the water companies have them installed only because it is cheaper than debt recovery. Households with these devices are actually charged more for water than normal, because of an 'administrative charge' added by the company. For example, North West Water adds 10p a week — that's £5.20 a year. Other costs may be incurred when travelling to and from outlets where the card can be charged.

Users have reported problems travelling to a place to charge the card — especially at weekends; and over a quarter couldn't find the money each week to charge the card.

Disconnection of the supply happens if credit runs out — and these disconnections do not show up in official figures. SevernTrent Water found that 49% of customers in a trial had been without water after running out of credit. Of those cut-offs longer than seven hours, 28% borrowed water — which is illegal under the Water Act. 18% stored it, incurring health risks, and 13% went without. The National Local Government Forum Against Poverty found that the majority of all those who are disconnected have children under five. The safety net is clearly failing them.

Ironically, many people with these devices use less water —
because they think they are paying for the volume they use. In fact
they provide no incentive at all to conserve water.

Such devices are on the increase; consumers should expect to
see more of them. Companies can seem to apply pressure upon
consumers to have them installed — but consumers don't have to.
It is important to remember that although they may be convenient
to use if you cannot meet a quarterly bill, they are really introduced
for the benefit of the company and its shareholders. It is ultimately
cheaper and perhaps easier, all things considered, just to put aside
£5 a week to pay the bill when it comes, if at all possible.

Selling water, making money

In the UK, under the 1995 Environment Act, water suppliers are
obligated to promote the efficient use of water. This duty is to be
enforced by Ofwat, but it is not clear how it will be interpreted.

On the face of it, it doesn't make sense for water companies to
promote water conservation. Companies do not make money by
promoting conservation and there is less profit for shareholders.

However, suppose we compare these utilities with the privatised electricity suppliers. Some of these have recently found it
beneficial to imitate the example of US suppliers and sell
electricity-saving appliances, such as low energy light bulbs, to
customers, because it is cheaper to do this than build new generating plants.

Some municipalities have taken similar innovative approaches
to household water conservation. New York City gives consumers
a rebate for replacing old toilets and showerheads with low-flow
models that covers two-thirds of the cost. The programme cost
$270 million and is predicted to defer or eliminate $8 to 12 billion
in water infrastructure expansion. The Canadian city of Waterloo
distributed free water-saving kits, containing low-flow shower
heads, aerators for taps, and toilet dams, to all households in the
summer of 1991. The result was a significant drop in water
consumption.

Should the UK water suppliers do the same thing? Our case
study of the Vales' roof rainwater collection (see page 110) shows

that it is possible to live easily on under half the budgeted amount of water per person per day in the UK (160 litres; the Vales use 35 litres but own a waterless toilet). The Vales notice no reduction in the quality of their life as a result. It may therefore may be cheaper for the companies to give incentives to customers to use less water — and indeed to supply them with equipment such as spray taps, showers and low-volume cisterns or waterless toilets, which would help both parties — than to invest in infrastructure changes such as the expensive replacement of leaky pipes. Selling water conservation devices at discount rates is one way. It may even make financial sense in certain areas for them to give such equipment away. However, as yet there is no sign that the companies are displaying this amount of imagination and enterprise. It is easier to put prices up.

Few customers will take the initiative alone to use less water (but we hope you will — see the next chapter!) — the incentive has to be provided by the water companies.

Chapter Six

Making do with less

Reducing Water Consumption in the Home

We have seen how 160 litres per person per day is the amount the authorities use to calculate supply. Do you actually use that much?

As a simple experiment one day, why not calculate how much you do use? Every time you turn on a tap or use a water-consuming appliance, measure the quantity, and at the end of the day add it up; perhaps if you have children they can help. You can then see for yourself where you can best make savings.

You probably know from doing the shopping how much a two litre bottle of water weighs. Imagine carrying all your daily water up a hill from a spring, as happens in some parts of the world. Wouldn't you cut down your use if you had to do this?

If everyone reduced their usage by only ten percent, then the water companies would be saved from making millions of pounds of investments. Such savings would be passed on to the consumer. We should also have fewer drought orders and the total environmental impact would be reduced.

Reduce, re-use, recycle

The general order of doing things is, reduce, re-use, recycle. In other words, before you consider recycling water, re-use it, and before you consider that, it's best just to reduce your consumption. In fact, recycling water is probably best avoided for most of us. Here is a 7-stage action plan for water reduction, going from the easiest to the hardest:

1. Develop an awareness of your water use and wastage.

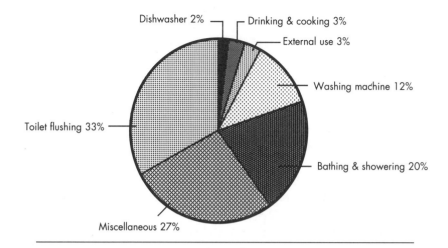

Dishwasher 2% — Drinking & cooking 3%
— External use 3%
Washing machine 12%
Toilet flushing 33% —
Bathing & showering 20%
Miscellaneous 27%

2. Plug leaks, dripping taps and cisterns.

3. Assess water use, and target possible savings.

4. Harvest rainwater for certain uses where purity is not necessary like in the garden and car washing.

5. Change or modify appliances.

6. Harvest rainwater for drinking purposes.

7. Recycle water.

Toilet flushing is the single biggest use of water in the home, accounting for 33% of household water use (see box). The majority of toilet cisterns in England and Wales use 9 litres per flush. Let's suppose you use the toilet eight times a day, that's 72 litres per person in a household. This water is expensively treated, just like that which we drink, but this is completely unnecessary merely to transport sewage to the treatment plants. The 1989 Water Bye-laws require that all new cisterns installed at the same time as a WC pan deliver no more than 7.5 litres of water per flush.

Dual flush toilets offer the option of a short flush or a long flush. The National Rivers Authority estimates that converting all domestic toilets to dual flush (around £7 from hardware stores — dual flush 9 or 7.5 litres) could save 850 million litres per day in England and Wales.

Low-flow models can be quite efficient — a good toilet depends more on the velocity of water flushing the pan than the volume of water used. If you can't afford to replace your toilet with a low-flow model, you can reduce the volume of the flush by installing toilet dams or placing a plastic bottle filled with water in the cistern (see diagram opposite). Compost toilets are the ultimate in water conserving models — they use no water at all. Small electric models exist which are only slightly larger than a normal toilet and use the same amount of electricity as a fridge. The deposits are heated to evaporate moisture and a fan extracts smells in some models. They fit in a conventional bathroom. The residue can be composted and used on the flower beds. Any environmental benefit they have, however, is offset by their consumption of electricity, which has implications for climate change and acid rain, besides cost. The choice is dependent on the circumstances and the user. Larger composting toilets are available which do not use electricity, but which do use more space, if you have such space in the relevant building available; these models are far more beneficial, with no environmental drawbacks. *Fertile Waste*, and *Sewage Solutions*, companion volumes in this series, (see Resource Guide) have lots of details on all types of dry toilets.

In the toilet and bathroom other steps can be taken to conserve and/or re-use water. Bathing and showering account for 20% of household water use. The average bath uses 80 litres; the average shower uses 30 litres. These figures obviously depend on the size of your bath and the length of your shower, but, generally speaking, showering is the better choice. Currently only a quarter of domestic properties are fitted with showers. If this is your situation, consider installing a shower attachment, make sure it has a flow restrictor and is not a water-guzzling 'power shower'.

You can install low-flow aerators or spray taps on any taps that have mains pressure water coming out — these attachments will use less water volume but give you just as much coverage as before. However, in most UK houses, only the kitchen tap and the washing machine are on mains pressure. The rest of the taps have low pressure water that comes from a storage tank in the attic. Low pressure taps generally use less water than a high pressure tap fitted with a low-flow aerator.

There are also systems available, like those used on trains, that allow you to use your knee or foot to turn on a tap only when you

Reducing your toilet flush

A plastic bottle filled with water will reduce the amount of water used for each flush. Be careful the bottle does not interfere with the ball cock mechanism. You should also be careful not to reduce your flow too much — depending on the design of your pan, you may need as much as 8 litres to flush effectively.

need it, leaving your hands free to wash or brush your teeth. These can save a lot of water by reducing the incentive to leave the tap running when you're not actually using the water. Ask your local plumber or plumbing supplier about these.

Water saving tips

GENERAL
- **Think twice:** much water conservation is common sense.
- **Check for leaks**, especially worn washers; mend or replace them.
- **Fit water conserving devices:** many commonly used appliances can be modified to conserve water or can be bought specifically for their water conserving design features. **Spray taps** and **faucet aerators** are an alternative to steady flow taps enabling a smaller volume of water to achieve the same results.

IN THE BATHROOM
- **use less water in a bath.**
- **low-flow shower heads** can be fitted to maximise water coverage and minimise water volume.

• By adding a sealed plastic bottle filled with water inside your toilet cistern, or by adjusting your ballcock, the amount of water used per flush can be reduced to a minimum. Alternatively a **dual flush toilet system** can be fitted which discharges a small volume of water for liquid waste and a larger volume for solid waste. Efficient flushing depends upon the velocity of the water rather than the volume, which tends to be grossly out of proportion to the waste that the water flushes he cistern increases efficiency. Double siphonic toilet pans are more effective than displacement flush pans. Consider installing a **dry toilet.**

IN THE KITCHEN

• **Washing clothes:** Use full loads in your washing machine, or if purchasing look for economy features such as half load capability or reduced water consumption.

• Conversely, **insulate hot water pipes** to prevent running the tap for long periods waiting for hot water.

• **Wash dishes by hand,** using one bowl for washing and one for rinsing. Bowls hold less water than it takes to fill the sink.

• **Compost** your vegetable waste instead of using a waste disposal unit.

• **Keep a jug of drinking water** in the fridge, so you avoid running the tap for long periods waiting for cold water.

• **Clean your veggies** in a bowl of water, not under a running tap.

• **Save your cooking water** and use as a stock or a base for soups; it can be kept for several days in a cooler or frozen.

OUTSIDE

• **Collect rainwater.** External use of water contributes to high demand in the summer. In most parts of the UK the water collected from rain falling on the roof of an average house could supply the water needs of at least one person, provided that the water is stored. This collected water can be used for most applications, but care should be taken if you suspect any leaching of particles from your roof surface. If this is the case then the water can still be used for washing your car or bicycle, and watering ornamental (non edible) plants. It is quite simple to collect rainwater in a butt placed under your downpipe and use it to water your garden. Also, it's probably better for your garden than chlorinated tap water. Keep the butt covered to prevent algae and insects from breeding in your store of rainwater. For convenience, you can fit a tap at the base of the butt. (For more elaborate rainwater systems, see 'Obtaining an Independent Supply'.)

- **Car washing:** don't use a hose. It is possible to wash a car with only two buckets of water — one of soapy water and one of rinsing water, if it's really necessary to clean it.
- **Garden watering:** to save water and to give your plants the maximum benefit it is best to water out of direct sunlight, e.g. in the evening. This will cut down on water loss due to evaporation. Avoid sprinklers, which use water indiscriminately, and try to target the water precisely where it is most needed. Grow plants in beds, not containers, and grow drought-resistant plants which don't need so much water. Infrequent, deep watering is better for your plants than frequent, shallow watering.
- **Recycle more:** all the water used in the home, apart from toilet-flush water, can be re-used to some degree. See below for detail.
- **Write to your local water company** and find out how much water it loses in its pipes through leakage and what measures it is taking to alleviate the situation. In some areas this figure is over one third. Demand to know why consumers should suffer shortages, rising costs and metering if the company will not plough more of its profits into conservation itself.

Re-using Wastewater
Household Greywater Recycling

'Blackwater' is what we call the highly polluted wastewater from toilets; 'greywater' is what we call water from everything else: sinks, bathtubs, washing machines, etc. Greywater is relatively clean: but it does contain significant quantities of grease, food waste, detergent and soap residues, hair, and other dirt. It rarely contains disease-causing organisms, unless you're washing dirty nappies.

On the face of it, it makes sense to re-use greywater for watering the garden or flushing the toilet, for example. In practice, it requires a fair bit of effort and may even be prohibited during droughts (because your wastewater may be needed as a source of water downstream). If you decide it's worth doing, keep the following points in mind:

- Fit a mesh filter on your plug hole — this will screen out the biggest particles.
- Use biodegradable cleaning products without additives if you plan to use your greywater for irrigation; avoid boron and bleach.
- Unless you want to rely on buckets or siphons, consider replumbing. You can fit a stopcock and hose spigot into the waste pipe that runs down the side of your house. Leave the stopcock open if you want it to drain normally, and close it when you want to divert a load of greywater to the garden. Replumbing to divert greywater to your WC cistern is much more work and probably not worth it unless you're installing an entire plumbing system.

Two cautions: fiddling with your drainage plumbing may not be allowed for health reasons — consult your Local Authority's Public Health Department. Secondly, don't try to store greywater — what you'll end up with is an unhealthy, smelly bacterial soup!

How much can you re-use? The average household produces 100 litres of greywater per person per day. If you plan to use it for irrigation — the most common form of re-use — figure that one square metre of soil can deal with approximately ten litres per week (more in the summer, less in the winter). Scale your <$igreywater re-use to suit your irrigation needs, and use the cleanest source first. This tends to be bath and shower water, followed by water from the bathroom sink, washing machine, utility sink, dishwasher and kitchen sink. If the volume of water from your bathtub is enough to water your garden, there is no need to worry about re-using that from the kitchen sink.

When it comes to irrigation, don't just throw your greywater on the garden. Unregulated dumping will mess up the soil structure, damage root hairs, and make clays more sticky and unworkable. And because soaps and detergents are rich in sodium, greywater can increase soil alkalinity. Some plants, like azaleas, conifers and rhododendrons, prefer acidic soil, so avoid watering them with greywater. The best approach is to rotate between different patches of soil — don't irrigate one spot exclusively or continuously. It's also a good idea to alternate between greywater and clean water. Finally, because there is a slight possibility that pathogens could be present, it is safest not to use greywater on food crops.

Chapter Seven

If you're not happy...

Only half of customers think the price they pay for tap water is reasonable and 39% think it is unreasonable. In addition, only a bit more than half (57%) are satisfied with the taste of their tap water. This is from a 1992 survey prepared for the Office of Water Services, Ofwat. In the same MORI survey, customers were asked to rank what standards in water they were most concerned with. Top of the league came safety — not surprisingly — then taste, appearance, sewage treatment and mains pressure.

So what do you do if you are dissatisfied about something?

All the water supply companies have a code of practice. Many publish and freely distribute a handbook which explains what services they offer and where your money goes. These all state that they want to know if you have any complaints or enquiries about the quality of your supply or your treatment as a consumer. And more and more people are responding to this request. As we have seen, the companies have to deal with millions of enquiries and complaints each year. This kind of feedback is extremely valuable for companies and for you, to help services improve.

How to proceed

If you are concerned about the quality of your water, you could start by finding out what's in it. You can get hold of the regional test results from your water company that will tell you if your water supply meets UK standards. Your local authority will also

─────────── Complaints ───────────

The percentage of complaints received by Ofwat's customer service committees in 1993/94, by category:

charges:	35.1%
billing:	24.2%
other:	16.3%
water supply:	12.2%
water quality:	5.8%
sewerage:	3.3%
water pressure:	3.1%

The total number of complaints received by Ofwat's Customer Service Committees, by year (these are only a small percentage of total consumer complaints as most people haven't heard of the CSCs):

1990/91:	4,613
1991/92:	10,638
1992/93:	14,795
1993/94:	14,302

supply them.

These results are put on public registers that will list all the parameters tested for, their maximum and average values, and the number of samples taken. Also it contains details of derogations (sometimes called 'relaxations' or 'undertakings', see pages 64-65) that allow the company to breach EC standards for particular substances. These are important: the more there are and the longer they last for, the more risk there has been from that particular substance.

You can visit your company's office or your town hall to look at the register, or request them to post the information to you. Copies of reports concerning the water in your area should be free, but you must pay for copies of reports about water in other areas. Your water company customer services staff will explain the results of the tests and tell you what is being done to rectify any failures.

The Drinking Water Inspectorate also publishes a leaflet called *About Your Water Company*. This gives a summary of information about the quality of drinking water supplied the previous year. It is taken from a lengthy report, which you can buy or may be able to see in a library, called *Drinking Water* (for the previous year). It is published by Her Majesty's Stationary Office, price £30.

If you have an emergency, contact your supplier first, using the number under 'Water' in the local phone book. Otherwise, use the general enquiry number, asking for customer services. You can also use this method to complain about charges and bills.

Your complaint should be dealt with in ten days (twenty days if it is about a bill, requires a visit, or requires further investigation). You are entitled to £10 compensation if your complaint is not dealt with in a timely fashion. If the result displeases you, you can:

- tell the relevant section of your local authority (all of UK);
- tell the environmental health officer at your local town hall (all of UK);
- tell the relevant section of the Department of the Environment (Scotland and Northern Ireland).
- contact the local Customer Service Committee of Ofwat. There are ten of these serving each region (England and Wales);
- finally, contact the Drinking Water Inspectorate (England and Wales).

In each case your concerns will be dealt with free of charge. Always keep records of any conversations or correspondence you have had, and the names of people you have talked to.

You can also get involved in groups that lobby for better water treatment. (For the contact details of all these organisations including the CSCs, see the Resource Guide. For more on the Customer Service Committees, see below.)

Testing your water

You can also have your tap water tested (see box overleaf). Home test kits are available, but these do not tend to be as comprehensive or accurate as analysis by a registered laboratory.

If there are problems with your water quality — high levels of heavy metals, for instance, or unpleasant tastes due to chlorine residuals — you might consider filtering your tap water. See 'Filter Systems' for details.

More on Consumer Rights

First, let's look at the Customer Service Committees. These have

Water sampling checklist

If you want to send your water for analysis, it is preferable to have a technician do the sampling and testing. However, if you have to do the sampling yourself, follow these steps carefully.

(1) select an indoor leak-free cold water tap

(2) if there is an aerator or strainer present, remove it

(3) sterilise the inside of the tap with a blow — torch, and don't contaminate it once it's sterilised

(4) let the water run at full flow for five minutes

(5) close the tap until the water is a stream the size of a pencil and let it flow for one minute

(6) fill a sterile, plastic if aluminium is to be tested, sample bottle to 3/4 capacity while holding the cap in your other hand, inner surface downwards — be careful not to contaminate either the bottle or the cap

(7) close the bottle immediately and label it

(8) deliver the sample to the lab for analysis as quickly as possible — it must get there within 30 hours at the very latest.

---

been set up by the Director General of Water Services, who is the supposedly independent economic regulator of the water and sewerage companies in England and Wales. He is part of Ofwat. The CSCs are, again, supposedly independent statutory bodies which are intended to represent the interests of householders and business customers. Each company is allocated by the Director General to one of the ten CSCs — which ones are allocated to which is listed in the Resource Guide. Their mission statement says that they are supposed to "secure for customers the combination of service and price that they would have in a competitive market". Of course, although the companies are privatised, there is no market, let alone a competitive one, because you can't exactly shop around for tap water. The statement also says that CSCs must make companies aware of and responsive to concerns about their services and ensure that companies have adequate complaints procedures. Finally, to quote Ofwat again: "It is vitally important that CSCs are seen to be independent of the water companies in their region and to be acting entirely in the public interest."

CSCs are examples of 'quangos' (i.e. quasi — non-governmental organisations). They consist of a chairperson, appointed by the Director General and the Secretary of State for Trade and Industry and the Secretary of State for Wales. They are handsomely paid, on a part-time basis, and work one or two days a week. Members of the CSCs however are unpaid, but can have their expenses reimbursed. They are appointed by the Director General and the chairperson. CSCs are hardly, then, models of democratic practice, and from this perspective it is clear that they need to do all they can to be seen to be independent and impartial. Ofwat says that "the key qualities required of members are an interest in and appreciation of consumer issues, an enquiring mind and sound judgement. Prior knowledge of the water industry and regulation are not essential." All sections of the community are supposed to be represented on a CSC; this includes minorities and low-income households; however they are also not supposed to be representatives of a particular interest group. If you feel strongly about your water and sewerage supply, and want to be considered as a member, then you can approach the CSC Appointment Unit at Ofwat (the contact details are in the Resource Guide).

In a recent survey (April 1996) half of people asked had never heard of Ofwat. If you compare the figures on page 88 — of the number of complaints dealt with by CSCs — against the total number of complaints received by the water companies (67 million over the same period), it means that less than 10% of customers who complain use the CSCs. It is likely that much less than a quarter of consumers even know of their existence. Perhaps also, as a quango, they are seen as being biased. Ofwat, too, is perceived as being remote and unconcerned with local people, according to the same survey by Trading Officers in the South West. Their report recommended that Local Authorities take over the role of consumer representation to the privatised utilities instead.

There is no national consumer group of water users, registered as a charity. The National Consumers Council does campaign about water and publishes helpful material (if you want to know what there is, their number is in the Resource Guide) — but there is no way it can devote a great deal of energy to this topic. The current opposition parties' spokespersons on water matters and their libraries are also a good source of information about the companies' behaviour and the parties are a route whereby political pressure may be exerted to regulate the industry further.

Chapter Eight

Alternatives to tap water

Many people buy bottled water or use water filters because they believe it is healthier than drinking tap water. Bottled and filtered waters are certainly dearer than tap water and they probably taste better, but they may not be significantly better for you.

Bottled Water

British consumers spend £1 million each day on bottled water, the fastest growing sector of the UK food and drinks industry. 30% of consumers currently drink bottled water.

There are more than 200 brands available in the UK, including still and sparkling varieties. Still waters contain no bubbles; they account for 60% of sales. Sparkling water is carbonated; it may be naturally bubbly, but more often has had carbon dioxide added.

Bottled water can be classified as natural mineral water, spring water, or table water.

According to EC and UK regulations, *natural mineral water* comes from an unpolluted underground source, is free from pathogenic organisms, and receives no treatment other than filtration to remove sand particles (see box). The term 'mineral' is somewhat misleading. They do not contain minerals in sufficient quantities to be actively good for you — and some brands actually sell themselves as being 'low in minerals' — often they are low, and they certainly don't compare to the levels of minerals you get in food. So this is not a reason to buy them!

————————*The great Perrier benzene scare*————————

In February 1990, Perrier discovered their famous bottled mineral water was contaminated with benzene, a colourless solvent known to cause cancer. After much panic, it turned out that their source was not affected; the problem was traced to a faulty gas line filter at the bottling plant. It was a costly mistake: Perrier withdrew all its stock from shop shelves — in Britain alone, this was 10 million bottles — and lost part of their market share as a result of the incident.

Spring water usually comes from an underground source, but it does not have to be bottled on the spot. It may receive treatment to alter its chemical make-up or remove disease-causing organisms. It is not currently regulated by specific legislation in the UK, but it must satisfy the Water Supply (Water Quality) Regulations 1989.

Table water is any that does not come from a single source. It may be a blend of different spring or mineral waters, and may even contain tap water. It is usually purified and may have mineral salts added to improve its flavour. Like spring water, it is not covered by specific legislation, but must meet drinking water standards.

The April 1991 issue of *Which?* reported on bottled water. Their expert panel sampled 29 brands but could not agree on overall favourites — preference was a matter of personal taste. Analysis of the waters found high nitrate levels in some brands (although still within permissible concentrations) and high levels of sodium and fluoride in one particular brand. Almost all the still waters contained high levels of bacteria.

Incidentally, it is not just for taste reasons that mineral waters are often served with a slice of lemon — lemon juice contains chemicals that are fatal to many bacteria. For a more extensive report on bottled water, see the *Good Water Guide* listed in the Resource Guide.

If you drink bottled water only occasionally, there's no need to be too concerned with reading labels. But if you consume it regularly, you should know what's in it. Most bottled waters give an analysis of their content on the label, and you can also write to the company and ask for more information. Look out for high levels of potassium — more than 12 mg/l can put stress on your kidneys. Magnesium sulphate and sodium sulphate are laxatives

—————EC Directive 777 (1980)—————

The following is an abridged version of the EC regulations governing natural mineral waters.

'Natural mineral water' is defined as microbiologically wholesome water, originating in an underground water table or deposit and emerging from a spring tapped at one or more natural or bore exits.

Authorised treatments are limited to the following:

(1) The separation of unstable elements (e.g. iron and sulphur) by filtration or decanting, which may be preceded by oxygenation.

(2) The elimination of carbon dioxide by exclusively physical methods.

(3) The addition of carbon dioxide according to definitions listed.

Effervescent mineral waters fall into three categories:

(1) 'Naturally carbonated mineral water', which contains the same carbon dioxide content as the source.

(2) 'Natural mineral water fortified with gas from the spring', which contains additional carbon dioxide to supplement its natural content.

(3) 'Carbonated natural mineral water', which naturally contains no carbon dioxide but has had carbon dioxide added.

At source and during its marketing, a natural mineral water shall be free from parasites and pathogenic micro-organisms, *E. coli* and other coliforms and faecal streptococci, sporulated sulphite-reducing anaerobes, and *Pseudomonas aeruginosa*.

The label must contain a composition analysis like the one here, the name of the spring, and its location.

Typical Analysis mg/l			
Calcium	5.3	Chloride	10.7
Magnesium	1.3	Sulphate	10.6
Sodium	5.1	Nitrate	0.2
Potassium	0.21	Nitrite	<0.1
Bicarbonate	28.1	Dry residue at 10^0	62
pH 6.5			

Best serve chilled
For best before date see top of bottle
Do not freeze

— don't use high-sulphate water when you're making baby formula. Finally, you should avoid waters with high sodium levels if you've been told to watch your sodium intake, and don't use them for making baby formula.

The Consumers' Association also urges that if you're using bottled water for baby formula, make sure you boil it first. Bottled water must be stored in the fridge after opening and consumed within three to four days. Don't drink directly from the bottle.

Generally, bottled water tastes better than tap water and filtered water, but costs 20p to 60p a litre, at least 600 times as much as tap water. Also, it may contain bacterial levels that are substantially higher than tap water. Finally, there are environmental costs associated with bottling water and trucking it long distances. Malvern Spring Water, for example, is exported to South America.

Filter Systems

Filter systems may improve the quality and taste of your tap water. Jug filters and in-line filters are available. The most popular type of system is the jug filter — these are used by 11% of the population, which itself says something about popular perceptions of water quality and taste, played upon by the marketing of such filters. The jug filters usually consist of a plastic two litre jug with a replaceable cartridge filter in the upper portion. You fill the top portion with tap water which is filtered as it trickles into the main portion of the jug.

Jug filters will usually remove most metals, organic substances, chlorine and water hardness. In February 1989, *Which?* magazine reported on several jug models: Addis Filtaware, Brita 'Fill and Pour', Leifheit Aquapur, Habitat, Waterboy, and Waymaster Crystal. All these used cartridges containing activated carbon and ion exchange resins. All removed lead, trichloroethylene and PAHs from both hard and soft water, and most removed iron and manganese from hard water. Only Waymaster Crystal was effective at reducing the level of nitrates, and then only when new.

Jug filters must be cared for properly to provide a safe supply of water (see box). Be aware: most filters remove chlorine residuals from tap water. Although chlorine residuals can give the water an unpleasant taste, they inhibit bacterial growth. Once you have filtered chlorine residuals out of the water, bacteria can grow quickly. For this reason, you should always store filtered water in the fridge. Also, filters must be replaced regularly — check the manufacturer's instructions. Overused filters can actually release

———————— Tips on the use of jug filters ————————

• always follow the manufacturer's instructions.
• don't leave water standing for several days — this encourages bacterial growth.
• keep filtered water in the fridge to discourage bacterial growth.
• clean the jug and reservoir weekly.
• don't keep a filter longer than advised by the manufacturer.

heavy metals and bacteria into your water.

Some filters are impregnated with silver, which acts as a disinfectant. However, it has only limited effectiveness, so you should still take precautions to reduce bacterial growth.

If you follow the manufacturer's instructions, filtering costs 3p to 7p per litre, excluding the initial cost of the jug. This works out to more than 60 times the cost of tap water, but it is ten times cheaper than bottled water.

Some people use filters to improve the taste of their tap water, even though the *Which?* panel found no real improvement in taste over tap water. If this is your reason for filtering and you can afford the cost, base your choice of system on taste. But if you're thinking of buying a filter to improve the quality of your tap water, find out what's in your water first (see 'If You're Not Happy' for details). Are there chlorine residuals? Too many heavy metals? Solvents? Buy a filter system that is designed to remove the particular contaminants you're concerned about. For example, if you are at risk from a high lead content in tap water and have children, then it is probably worth investing in a filter.

You might also consider 'in-line' or 'point of use' filter systems that can be installed under your sink to treat larger volumes of water. These offer more convenience than jug filters — you just turn on your tap to get filtered water instead of constantly refilling jugs. They do cost substantially more than jug filters, although the filters do not have to be replaced as frequently. See the following chapter for a discussion of point-of-use filters systems in the context of private water supplies. You can also consult the *Which?* report on using in-line systems to treat tap water in its August 1990 issue.

Chapter Nine

If you're not on the mains...

These days, most people in the UK are connected to the mains. In England and Wales, only 1% of the population has private water supplies: approximately 10,000 properties are connected to private supplies, compared to 22.4 million properties connected to the mains. The numbers of private supplies are somewhat higher in Scotland and Northern Ireland.

Private supplies are governed by the Private Water Supplies Regulations 1992 in England and Wales, and by the Private Water Supplies (Scotland) Regulations 1992 in Scotland. Maintenance and repair of the supply is the responsibility of the owner or user. In England and Wales, monitoring is the responsibility of the local authorities; in Scotland, the new Water Authorities; and in Northern Ireland, the Department of the Environment. The quality of private supplies intended for domestic uses or food production purposes must meet standards set out in the UK Regulations.

This chapter describes how to collect water from various sources, how to store and disinfect it, and how to treat it. Some of this can be done yourself if you have the basic skills, some of it will require a specialist contractor.

Obtaining an Independent Supply

If you want an independent supply, the basic requirements to keep in mind are adequate quantity, adequate quality, and acceptable cost. There are three potential sources of water to choose from: groundwater, surface water and direct rainwater.

First of all, calculate how much water you'll need. A potential water source should provide you with a reliable volume of water sufficient to meet all your needs — enough to supply your daily household needs, garden and livestock. Plan on at least 140 litres per person per day, 5 litres of which will be used for cooking and drinking. Of course, it's relatively easy to reduce the amount of water you use around the house (see 'Reducing Water Consumption'), but at this point you're better off to overestimate your needs than to underestimate them. Don't forget about guests! You should also take droughts into account — allow for a minimum of 14 days without an external supply to the tank. Groundwater is the most reliable source of water, if your well is deep enough.

A potential source should also provide you with raw water that is reasonably clean. It is usually easier and cheaper to use good quality water that is more difficult to abstract than to treat polluted water that is easier to obtain. In terms of purity, groundwater is preferable to surface water. The initial costs of accessing a groundwater source are high, but the water you get will probably require much less treatment than water from other sources. If you choose surface water, water sources from upland areas are preferable to those from lowland areas (provided the upland area is not peaty or used for agricultural purposes). Keep in mind that clean water is vital to your health — it's not worth taking risks to save a few pounds.

Finally, check the legalities of using the source. In England and Wales, you need a license for most types of abstraction. Contact your local region of the National Rivers Authority and ask for an abstraction license application package.

Groundwater

The biggest problem with using groundwater is finding it in the first place. You'll need to have some test holes drilled to discover how far down the water is, how much there is, and how good the quality of it is. Check your Yellow Pages for a contractor who will do this initial assessment. A dowser may also be helpful in choosing the best places to drill test holes. To find one contact the

British Society of Dowsers, listed in the Resource Guide.

Wells and Boreholes

Groundwater is abstracted through holes in the ground called wells or boreholes. A well has a diameter greater than one meter and is dug by hand or mechanical excavation. The walls are made of impermeable brick or cement, and the water comes up through a layer of sand at the bottom of the shaft (see diagram opposite, top).

A borehole is smaller and deeper than a well. It is drilled by a contractor with special equipment. The borehole is lined with a perforated steel shaft, and water flows in through the holes (see diagram opposite, bottom).

Wells and boreholes can be classified by depth. Shallow wells or boreholes abstract water from water-bearing rocks above the first impermeable layer (see diagram, page 102). These are less reliable and can dry up during droughts. Deep wells or boreholes abstract water from water-bearing rocks below an impermeable layer. They provide a more reliable supply and are less likely to be contaminated.

There are many different types of wells and boreholes: dug, bored, driven, jetted or drilled, described in detail later. Which type you choose will depend on the resources you have available, the type of soil you'll need to dig through, and how far you'll need to dig to hit a reliable source of water.

If there's water close to the surface, you can dig a well with a JCB and then line it with cement rings or brick. Or, if the soil is soft enough, you can dig it by hand. Take a concrete ring — say 90 cm in diameter — and place it on the ground. Stand inside the ring and start digging. As you remove the earth, the concrete ring will move down. Eventually, when the top of the first ring is level with the ground, you mortar a second ring on top and continue digging. Keep digging and adding rings until you're well into the water table. Then line the bottom of the well with a layer of sand e.g. 0.5m.

If the water is further down, you'll probably need to hire a contractor with specialised drilling equipment. This will cost a few thousand pounds, but will produce a deeper well that is less likely

Wells and boreholes

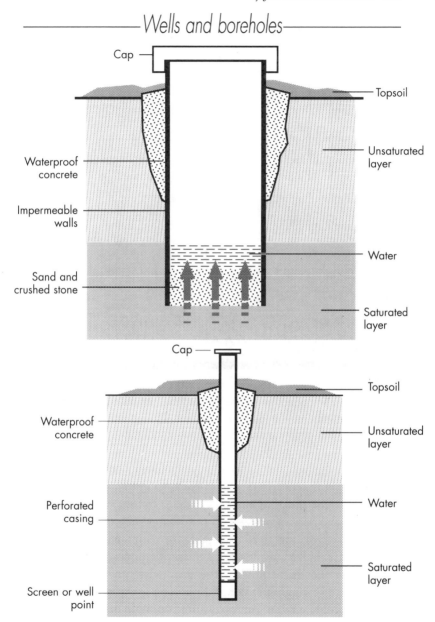

Wells (top) are much wider than boreholes and frequently more shallow. Water enters a well from the bottom, often through a layer of sand and crushed stone. Water enters a borehole through the perforated casing.

Classification of wells by depth

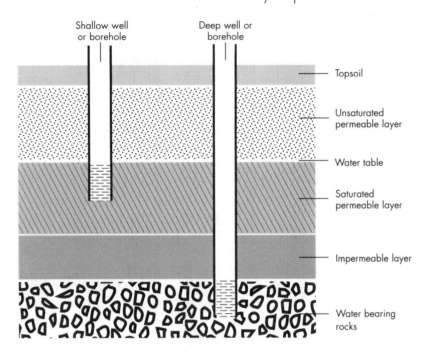

Shallow well
or borehole

Deep well or
borehole

Topsoil

Unsaturated
permeable layer

Water table

Saturated
permeable layer

Impermeable layer

Water bearing
rocks

Shallow wells and boreholes are less reliable than deep ones, because they can dry up if the water table drops.

to become contaminated, and will give a more reliable supply.

Before you begin to dig, check the regulations. Locate the well to minimise the threat of surface drainage getting into the well, to encourage the flow of possible groundwater pollutants away from the water source, and to be accessible for maintenance and repair. In particular, make sure it's not near septic tanks and leachfields. Dig during the driest time of the year when the water table is lowest to make digging easier and reduce pumping costs.

To prevent surface run-off from contaminating your water supply, make sure there's at least 20 cm of casing emerging from the ground. Seal around the casing with waterproof concrete. Keep the well or borehole securely covered, and don't let in any light — this will discourage algae and other micro-organisms from growing in your water supply.

Once it's built, you'll need a pump to get the water from the well. For a borehole, choose a submersible pump that sits inside the borehole below the water level. For a well, there are several choices. You could use a submersible pump, an in-line pump (located on the supply pipe), or a hand bucket. An in-line pump has the advantage that it's more accessible for repairs.

When you call your supplier, you should know the volume of water you'll want to pump each hour, the head (i.e. the height difference between your supply and your storage tank) and the bore of the pipe through which you'll be pumping the water. The supplier can then advise you on the best model for your needs.

Finally, you'll need to disinfect your well or borehole. This is not the same thing as the ongoing process of disinfecting your water supply — it is a one-time job to clean the well or borehole itself. The easiest way to do it is with chlorine tablets (calcium hypochlorite) which you can get from your local contractor. Drop them down the well, let the chlorinated water sit for 24 hours, then pump out all the chlorinated water (you'll know when you're finished when the water stops smelling of chlorine). Now you're ready for business.

If you choose to hire a contractor, all this work will probably be done for you. A contractor will generally take care of everything from drilling, installing the well casing, sealing the well, pumping it, and disinfecting it, up to piping the untreated water to your house. All you would be responsible for is setting up the treatment system and connecting the supply to your household plumbing.

Well maintenance is not a lot of work. You should check the water level periodically to make sure it's not going down, and check that the well seal and connection are intact and protected from surface drainage.

Types of wells
Dug

These wells are dug by hand. The bottom is covered with gravel and the walls are lined with bricks, stones or culverts. They can be up to 15 metres deep and range in diameter from 8 to 10 cm. They are suitable for clay, silt, sand, gravel, boulders, soft sandstone, and soft fractured limestone; they are not suitable for dense igneous rock. There are a couple of disadvantages to dug wells: they tend to have low yield and can run dry in the summer, and they are difficult to protect from pollution.

Bored

These are deeper than dug wells (up to 30 metres) and lined with tiles, concrete pipe, wrought iron or steel casing. Diameters range from 5 to 75 cm. Like dug wells, they are suitable for clay, silt, sand, gravel, boulders smaller than the diameter of the well, soft sandstone, and soft fractured limestone; they are not suitable for dense igneous rock. They are also susceptible to pollution and may not provide a reliable supply of water.

Driven

This is the least expensive and simplest type of well to construct. A special well point is attached to a steel pipe and driven into the ground. Driven wells can be up to 15m deep and 3 to 5cm in diameter. They are suitable for clay, sand, fine gravel, and sandstone in thin layers; and unsuitable for cemented gravel, boulders, limestone, or dense igneous rock. Like dug and bored wells, they can be prone to pollution and may not provide a reliable supply.

Jetted

Jetting is quick and effective in soft, loose soil. Water is forced down a drill pipe by a pressure pump and out through holes in the drill bit, pushing cuttings to the surface through the space between the casing and the drill pipe. Jetted wells are up to 30 metres deep and 10 to 30 cm in diameter. They are suitable for clay, silt, sand, and small pea gravel; they are not suitable for cemented gravel, boulders, sandstone, limestone, or dense igneous rock.

Drilled

Drilled wells provide the safest and most reliable supply of water and are excavated using machine-operated drilling rigs or equipment. Suitable for clay, silt, gravel, cemented gravel, boulders (in firm bedding), sandstone, limestone, and dense igneous rock,

Spring boxes

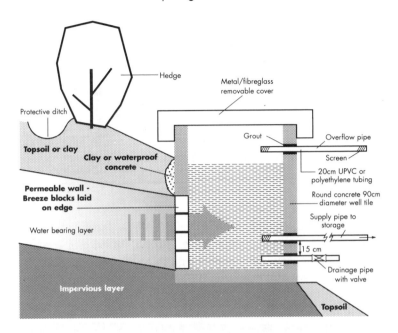

A spring box will protect your spring from contamination. The box is built into the hillside, with a permeable rear wall that allows the water to flow in. A protective ditch and hedge are located above the box to divert surface run-off.

they can be up to 300 metres deep and 10 to 60 cm in diameter.

Springs

Groundwater can also be obtained from a spring — a point where groundwater flows out of a crack in the aquifer to the surface. Some springs are reliable all year-round, others can dry up after short periods without rain. Make sure your spring is reliable before you decide to use it as your water supply.

Springs must be protected from pollution. A shelter will ensure that water flows directly from the spring into your pipe without the opportunity for contamination (see diagram above). After the shelter is built you should disinfect it with chlorine tablets. Then the only maintenance required is cleaning out the silt once a year.

—————— *CASE STUDY: Spring source* ——————

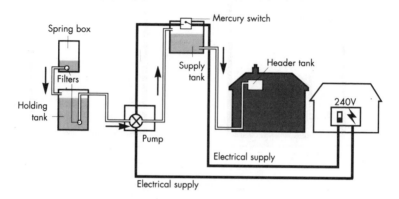

Esgair Fawr is a cottage in the Welsh hills with its own water supply drawn from a spring on the wooded hillside above the house. The spring emerges at the point where the rainwater which has fallen on the hill above, percolating down through permeable rock, comes to a layer of impermeable rock and is forced out to the surface. As the schematic diagram shows, a brick and concrete box was built around the spring to protect it and the water is is filtered off and collected in a holding tank/cistern. An electric pump housed adjacent to the holding tank sends water to a supply storage tank 25m above from where the water is fed by gravity to the house lower down.

Electrical supply to the pump is delivered from an outbuilding via armoured cable beneath the ground. From the pump it travels on up to the supply tank

Surface Water

Surface water comes in a variety of forms: streams, rivers, ponds, and lakes. Before selecting a potential water source, consider if the water quality is acceptable. Are there sources of contamination upstream? Farms are one of the biggest sources of contamination, through run-off of fertilisers, pesticides and animal wastes. Industrial effluent and sewage outfalls are other obvious sources of pollution, but also check for abandoned mines. You may need to get it tested (see 'If you're not happy...'). Finally, how reliable is the source? Will it dry up in summer? How much water

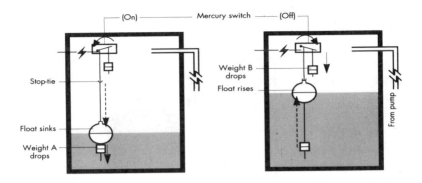

where a mercury switch is located. The switch forms the on/ off break in the supply before it returns to the outbuilding, completing the 'loop'. This ingenious switch is designed to 'know' when to, and when not to, pump to the cottage. A glass vial containing mercury, attached to a rocking 'see-saw' mechanism is housed in a waterproof box, fitted to the inner wall at the top of the supply tank just below the lid. It is activated by weights suspended below (see the figure above). The level of water in the supply tank determines whether the switch is on or off. When the water level in the supply tank drops, so does the free moving ball float. As the float sinks it eventually meets weight (A). As the water level drops further the weight of the float 'tips' the vial, causing an electrical contact and switching the pump on. As the water rises, so does the ball float, until it reaches a set level governed by an adjustable stop-tie. Further increase in the level of water now forces the float against the stop-tie causing weight (B) to drop, 'tipping' the switch off .Maintenance generally consists of keeping everything clean and free of debris.

---

will be lost through evaporation and seepage?

To obtain water from a surface source, you may need to dam the supply, or you may simply be able to stick a 25mm bore pipe into the source to carry the water to a storage facility below. The intake pipe should be covered by a mesh screen to prevent leaves, twigs and assorted aquatic life from getting into your supply. You can construct a bulb out of wire mesh and stick it on the end of the pipe — this is less likely to get clogged up by a few leaves than a flat screen would be.

Make sure the pipe is fixed firmly in place to prevent it from

—————————*CASE STUDY: Surface water*—————————

The Centre for Alternative Technology is situated on the site of an old slate quarry, whose cutting machines were originally water-powered. In the middle of the last century the valley above the site was dammed with slate and soil, and a reservoir created. This is the source of the majority of the Centre's hydropower and drinking and service water. The reservoir is fed by two streams which originate in unimproved rough upland pasture. Apart from a few suspended solids and some faecal coliforms from sheep, there is no other contamination of any sort.

The original extraction pipes have corroded and are buried in silt. Water is now siphoned out over the dam in a 200mm diameter pipe, which runs down the hillside for 200 metres, although the drop in height is only 10 metres. All pipework is alkathene. At this point a 63mm diameter pipe is T'd off to supply all the drinking and service water. The remaining flow descends a further 20 metres vertical height down to the site, where it is used to run a water turbine.

The flow rate in this pipe is 19 litres per second, and the usable capacity of the reservoir is around 5 million litres, which ensures a few days' storage for the system. Sufficient water is always left in the reservoir for drinking purposes.

The 63mm pipe is sub-divided and a 25mm pipe T'd off to feed a slow sand filter (like the one illustrated on page 110) which provides all the site's drinking water. The filter is two-chambered and has a surface area of approximately 4m². After filtration, the water is stored in three 1500 litre containers, to cope with the variable demand. This clean supply then descends to the site in a 63mm pipe where it is distributed to the restaurant, domestic properties and other facilities.

An ultra-violet filter provides further treatment for the restaurant and other public supplies to ensure the water meets Environmental Health standards. The unfiltered supply descends directly to the site and provides water for the gardens, toilet flushing and fire hydrants.

By splitting the water supply, the Centre has reduced its demand for filtered water by over 75%. The unfiltered supply has an increased pressure of 3 bar, whereas the filtered supply is comparable to mains supplies at 2 bars. This added pressure is enjoyed by the gardeners.

washing away. The mouth of the pipe should be well above the river bottom so that it's in no danger of being silted up or buried, but well below the water surface. A rocky site is your best bet.

Rainwater

Rainwater is readily available and easy to collect from your roof. It can accumulate a lot of contaminants though, both from pollution in the air and from the surface it falls on. It tends to contain high levels of bacteria. It's not a good idea to rely on rainwater in polluted urban areas, because the rain will pick up a lot of contaminants from the air, particularly hydrocarbons, which are difficult to remove. Also, because it depends directly on rainfall, it is not as reliable as other sources. However, having said this, our case study demonstrates it can be done effectively (see pp.110 — 111).

To estimate how much water you can collect, you need to know your annual rainfall and the collecting area of your roof. Don't be fooled — the collecting area is not the number of square metres of roofing, but the 'footprint' of your roof — the number of square metres it would occupy if it sat directly on the ground. Figure that you can collect 0.8 litres for every one millimetre of rain that falls on a square metre of roof collecting area. So to calculate your average daily yield, use the following formula:

[annual rainfall (mm/year) x collecting area of roof (m^2) x 0.8 (l/mm/m^2)] ÷ 365 days/year = average l/day.

An example may help. Let's use the figures from the case study of the Vales' system on the following page. The annual rainfall, 600mm, times the 140m^2 collecting area, times 0.8, works out as 67,200; divided by the days of the year, makes 184 litres per day. The Vales use 140 litres a day so that provides plenty of leeway.

To prevent contamination, make sure all the surfaces the rain will contact are clean, smooth and non-toxic. Rough surfaces collect dirt and debris that will wash off with the rain. Thatched roofs are not ideal for collecting rainwater. Make sure your gutter and downpipe system is made of materials approved for potable water systems. Although standard PVC pipes and gutters are fine, copper is best, which is why it's used in domestic systems. Cover

CASE STUDY: Rainwater Collection

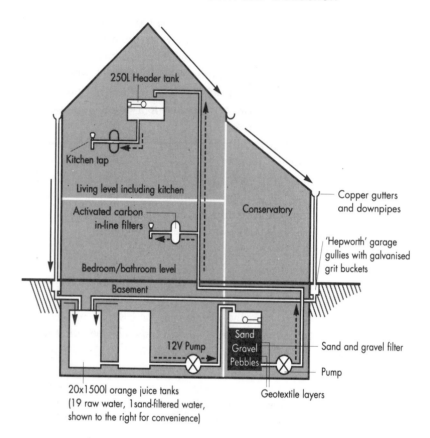

250L Header tank

Kitchen tap

Living level including kitchen

Activated carbon
in-line filters

Bedroom/bathroom level

Basement

12V Pump

Sand
Gravel
Pebbles

Conservatory

Copper gutters
and downpipes

'Hepworth' garage
gullies with galvanised
grit buckets

Sand and gravel filter

Pump

20x1500l orange juice tanks
(19 raw water, 1 sand-filtered water,
shown to the right for convenience)

Geotextile layers

Robert and Brenda Vale live in a self-sufficient house in Southwell, Nottinghamshire. They had the house built themselves to their own design for £150,000 in 1993. It has its own power supply (photo-voltaic cells) and sewage system (waterless toilet) and for its water supply relies on roofwater collection of rainfall. Despite the fact that there is only 600mm a year rainfall, they manage perfectly well — at the height of the 1995 drought, their tanks were still two thirds full. This is because, even with daily showers for a family of four and very occasional car washing, they use 'only' an average of 35 litres per person per day, by applying standard water conservation measures.

The water is collected from the roofs of the house and conservatory, which together have a plan area of 140m². The roof has traditional clay pantiles and glass for the conservatory, which drain to copper gutters and downpipes. Copper was chosen for its low toxicity; PVC is extruded with lead, copper has a slight anti-bacterial effect, which is why it is used in household plumbing, and they were advised that the UK diet is low on copper anyway! These drain to 'Hepworth' garage gullies with galvanised grit buckets in them to act as coarse strainers — "We fish out the leaves and dead pigeons every now and then," joked Robert. In the substantial basement, there are 19 1,500 litre tanks — actually Israeli orange juice containers — bought from a local tank supplier found in the Yellow Pages. These are linked together as shown in the diagram — 100mm above ground level, to allow for sedimentation — so they all fill simultaneously. There is an overflow to a soakaway through a 6mm drilled stainless steel plate.

The tanks feed via a 12V 'Shurflo' pressure switched pump to a sand and gravel filter (made from another Israeli storage tank), and from there to a 20th storage tank. The filter tank can be filled up to 70mm above the sand level. When the pump is switched on by the ballcock on the storage tank it pulls the water through the filter.

When the taps are turned on, a second 12V pump sends water up the rising main to the 250 litre header tank. This is tapped half way up for the drinking water in the kitchen, because the ceramic, activated carbon in-line filter needs to be pressure fed. There is no UV treatment. A further drinking water tap is fed from the header tank via another in-line filter. The whole system is therefore demand-led.

The system has been used continuously, with no other supply, since November 1993.

"Over and above the cost of normal plumbing, I reckon it cost £2,500 — including £1,800 for the tanks," says Robert. "But when you consider the water company charges £1,500 for joining to the mains, that's only £1000 more than normal."

Rainwater cistern

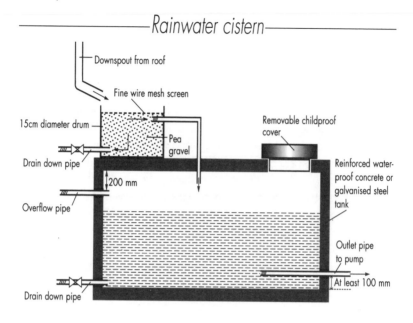

The filtering box directly underneath the downpipe collects the first flush of rainwater, which can contain a lot of contaminants. Once the box is full, water flows across the top of this and into the main tank, where it is stored before treatment. After a rainfall, the filtering box should be drained out.

your gutters with screen or mesh to prevent leaves from blocking them up, and use a screening tank before storage.

Rainwater can be collected in a cistern underneath the downspout (see diagram above). The size of your cistern will be determined by the volume of water you will need to survive for four weeks without rain. Disinfect the cistern with chlorine tablets after it's been installed. You should always divert the first flush of rainwater from the cistern, through a filtering box for example.

Rainwater is soft. It's good for bathing, laundry and dishwashing, but it is not as healthy to drink as hard water. To make it suitable for drinking, you can add calcium carbonate to your supply to harden it. A lump of chalk rock about the size of your fist will do the trick, or you can buy commercial hardeners.

Sample household storage system

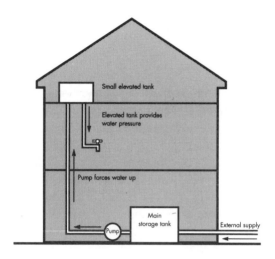

Small elevated tank

Elevated tank provides
water pressure

Pump forces water up

Main
storage tank

Pump

External supply

In a typical household storage system, the main storage tank is located in the cellar. A portion of the water is pumped up to an elevated tank in the attic to create water pressure at the taps.

Storing and Distributing Your Supply

Storing water serves two functions: it buffers differences between supply and demand, and, if the water store is higher than your tap, it can produce pressure in the system.

The size of your storage tank will depend on demand — see the discussion at the beginning of 'Obtaining an Independent Supply'. It must be able to meet your peak demand (probably half of your total daily requirement is used during a few peak hours).

The mains pressure at conventional taps is approximately 1.5 bar, with a flow rate of 0.5 litres per second, but you can probably get by with a little less. 600 vertical millimetres equals 1 p.s.i. of pressure; so to create mains pressure, which is supposed to be 20 p.s.i., you would need to raise your water up 12 metres. But water is heavy, and most houses are not structurally designed to support large tanks of water in the attic. You could use a pump to create pressure directly, but the more efficient method is to have your main storage tank at or below ground level, and use a pump to raise some of it up to a smaller tank in the attic (see diagram on page 113).

Storage tanks should be made of a clean, inert and non-porous material, for example bricks with an impervious render, ferro-cement with render, or plastic containers (plastic barrels used commercially for fruit juice are a good choice). The tank should be covered, but easily accessible.

Piping can be steel, PVC, copper or polythene. The size of bore will depend on how much water you're dealing with. In rough terms, the pipes that deliver water from your source to a storage tank should have a 25mm to 19mm bore; the pipes that move water from storage tank to storage tank should have a 6mm to 8mm bore; and pipes that deliver stored water to your tap should have a 1-2mm bore.

To complete your system you'll probably want a float switch to switch the pump on when water levels become too low and off when water levels become too high, or a pressure-operated pump that switches on in response to reduced pressure when you turn on the tap.

Making It Drinkable

The degree of treatment your water supply will require depends on the quality of the raw water and on what you intend to use the treated water for. You should have the raw water tested initially to decide what treatment is required, then, once the treatment system is operating, test the treated water to make sure the treatment is effective. You should also have your water tested every two to three years (or immediately if you notice a dramatic change in taste, odour or colour). If you go to a private laboratory for testing, it's worth shopping around for a good price. All laboratories must meet universal standards of reliability, but the prices they charge can vary considerably.

Generally speaking, groundwater is high quality water and does not require much in the way of treatment. Surface water requires more extensive treatment because it can be polluted by

A simple slow sand filter

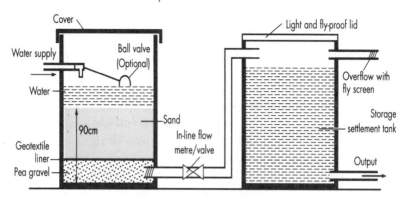

This simple filter works on the principle of slow sand filters in municipal water treatment plants. The water is filtered by the sand itself, and by the layer of micro-organisms that develops on top of the sand. A nylon curtain makes a good geotextile liner.

various sources. As a minimum, it should be filtered and disinfected, but base your treatment regime on the worst expected raw water quality. Rainwater can also be quite polluted, so disinfection is essential.

It may be worth installing two separate water systems: one for high quality potable water, and one for lower quality water for non-potable purposes. This can save you money on treatment, but will require a dual plumbing system.

Storage can be useful for killing bacteria, and storing untreated watercan allow bacteria, etc to grow, therefore treat water before storage and then again just before use, especially drinking water.

There are two broad categories of water treatment: point of entry treatment and point of use treatment. Point of entry systems are suitable for large private water supplies (i.e. small communities); point of use systems are best for individual household supplies.

Point of Entry Treatment

Point of entry systems treat water near the source. The system you choose will depend on the quality of your raw water.

You can build yourself a basic slow sand filter that will remove most bacteria, insoluble organic pollutants, and suspended solids. (see diagram, overleaf). Choose a container with a rough interior (for example, concrete blocks rendered on the inside) to prevent water from running down the sides without being filtered. Then fill it with layers of particles starting with pea gravel and finishing with very fine sand (you can often find sharp sand intended for cement at building merchants that is suitable). You should end up with a depth of 90 cm. Once it's in use, a layer of algae and other organisms will begin to grow on top of the sand. This is the 'schmutzdecke' and it helps to filter the water. Maintenance is very simple: the *schmutzdecke* and the first few centimetres of sand must be cleared off every few months when it starts to clog things up, and the sand should be topped up every five to six years so it's always 90 cm deep. A 1m² sand filter will treat enough water for four to ten people. Don't build one smaller than this, though — if it's smaller than 1m², it won't work effectively.

If you fit an in-line flow meter and valve on the outlet pipe, you can monitor the water flow. Ideally the flow should be 0.1 cubic metres of water per m² of sand per hour to ensure good treatment. When it drops below this flow rate, open the valve a little more. When the valve is fully open and the flow is less than 0.1 l/m²/hr, it's time to clear off the *schmutzdecke*. Make sure there's always water trickling through the filter — it's not a good idea to let the sand dry out.

It's a good idea to use an in-line micro filter after the sand filter to catch sand particles that might wash out in the filtered water and cause wear and tear on your plumbing and fixtures.

If your raw water is relatively clean, the slow sand filter may be all you need. If your water is very silty or cloudy, you should settle out the suspended particles in a simple settling tank located before the sand filter. If there's lots of bacteria in the raw water, you should take the precaution of disinfecting the water after it's been filtered. You can buy UV disinfection units or automatic chlorinators off-the-shelf for this purpose.

Point of Use Treatment
These off-the-shelf systems are appropriate for generating

relatively small volumes of drinking water. They can be used to treat a private water supply, or to improve the quality of mains water. Different models are available: some are installed before the tap, some connect directly to the tap, and some stand separate from the plumbing system. Many point of use systems are connected to a UV disinfection unit to kill any bacteria remaining after filtration. Choose the system that will remove the specific contaminants your incoming water contains (see table overleaf and individual descriptions), but keep in mind that a point-of-use system may not be adequate if the incoming water is so contaminated that it does not meet bathing standards. Unfortunately, British Standards have not been established for home treatment systems.

Particulate Filters

These are used to reduce turbidity or remove specific inorganic particulates such as iron, aluminium or manganese compounds. Particles and bacteria may also be removed, depending on pore size. There are several different types available: disc, woven or resin bonded cartridges, and ceramic candles. Bacteria may grow on particulate filters, so there is a danger they could contaminate the treated water. Some filters are impregnated with silver to prevent or inhibit bacterial growth.

Capital costs for a particulate filter system range from £30 to £300 (the more expensive units include a built-in UV disinfection unit); replacement filters cost £6 to £12.

Activated carbon filters

Activated carbon filters work by physically absorbing contaminants onto the surface of carbon particles. They can improve the taste and odour of your water by removing certain industrial wastes, pesticides, decaying organic material, dissolved gases, residual chlorine and by-products of chlorination. They will also remove (to varying degrees) suspended solids, turbidity and organic contaminants. There are two basic types: cartridge filters and activated carbon bed filters.

The cartridge models can fit on a tap or mount under the sink. The activated carbon is contained in replaceable cartridges — granular activated carbon is most common, but powdered

──────Comparison of point of use systems──────

— effectiveness at removing contaminants

	particulate filters	activated carbon filters	reverse osmosis units	ion exchange units	UV disinfection units
suspended solids	yes	some	yes	no	no
hardness	no	no	yes	yes	no
nitrates	no	no	yes	yes	no
lead	no	no	yes	yes	no
bacteria & viruses	most	some	yes	no	yes
chlorinated organic compounds	no	yes	yes	some	no
tastes & odours	no	yes	yes	some	no
initial expense	£30-300	£30-300	£150-600	£25-500	£200
new filters	£6-12	£8-18			£18

activated carbon and block carbon can also be used. A particulate filter at the outlet of the cartridge removes carbon particles from the treated water.

The bed model is designed to treat large volumes of household water (see diagram on page 119). It is placed after the disinfection unit and the water softener, if these are present. Activated carbon bed filters must be backwashed periodically.

One concern about activated carbon filters is that, by removing chlorine residuals, they may encourage the growth of bacteria — some studies have shown that water leaving a point of use activated carbon filter system may contain more bacteria than untreated water. To prevent this, some filters are impregnated with silver; others are close-coupled to a UV disinfection unit.

Capital costs are £30 to £300 (the more expensive units include a built-in UV disinfection unit); replacement cartridge filters are £8

Activated carbon bed filter

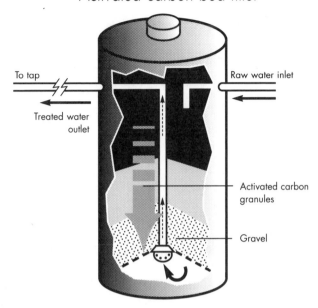

To tap

Treated water outlet

Raw water inlet

Activated carbon granules

Gravel

Activated carbon bed filters are often fitted underneath the sink. The activated carbon granules remove contaminants as the water filters through. The treated water then goes directly to the tap.

to £18. Filters will probably need replacing twice a year.

Pre-coat activated carbon filters

These systems are similar to activated carbon filters, but instead of using granular carbon, they use powdered carbon. They provide more effective filtration. Like other filter systems, they may encourage bacterial growth by removing chlorine residuals, if present.

Capital costs are £30 to £40.

Reverse osmosis units

Reverse osmosis will remove (to varying degrees) dissolved inorganic contaminants such as sodium, calcium, nitrates and fluoride, and organic contaminants, including pesticides and solvents. The functional basis of a reverse osmosis unit is a semi-

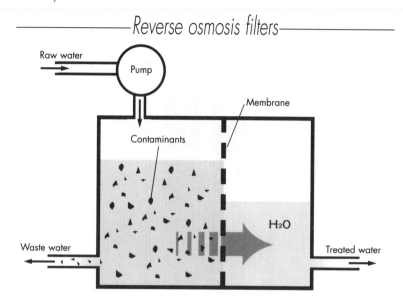

Reverse osmosis filters

The active ingredient of a reverse osmosis unit is a semi-permeable membrane that allows water but not contaminants to pass through. Pressure created by the pump pushes water across the membrane.

---

permeable membrane, usually made of polyamide, that allows water but not other molecules to pass through (see diagram above). A high pressure pump pushes water through the membrane at a force of 14 to 29 bar. Salts, minerals, dirt particles, bacteria and viruses are trapped by the membrane. Incoming water constantly cleans the membrane, and contaminants are washed out in the 'reject' water.

There are several drawbacks to reverse osmosis systems. The incoming water must be of good quality to prevent the membrane from scaling and fouling. The membrane itself must be chemically cleaned and replaced every few years. Flow rate is very slow, so the treated water must be collected in a storage tank to buffer supply and demand. The treated water is often soft and acidic, making it unhealthy to drink. Finally, for every one volume of clean water produced by the system, three volumes are wasted as 'reject' water.

The capital cost of a reverse osmosis system is £150 to £600 (the

Water softeners

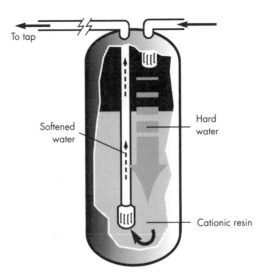

Water softeners work by exchanging calcium and magnesium ions that cause hardness with sodium ions. The exchange occurs in the cationic resin, which must be recharged periodically with saline solution.

more expensive units include a built-in UV disinfection unit).

Ion exchange units

Ion exchange units do not purify water *per se*, but they can soften hard water or remove nitrates. These systems use synthetic resins — small beads 0.2 to 2.0 mm in diameter. They can be cationic or anionic. Cationic resins soften water by exchanging positively charged calcium and magnesium ions with sodium (see diagram). Softened water should only be used for washing; it is not healthy to drink water that is too soft. Anionic resins exchange negatively charged nitrates with chloride ions.

When the resins are exhausted, they can be regenerated with sodium chloride solution. The capital cost of a cationic unit ranges from £25 for a replaceable cartridge model to £500 for a fully regenerable model. Anionic exchange units cost £25 to £250.

Ultraviolet disinfection units

Known as UV units for short, these will disinfect your water supply — they kill micro-organisms that could cause disease. However, they won't remove anything else that might be in the water, such as suspended particles, metals or chlorinated organic compounds, and they won't solve taste or odour problems.

UV systems comprise of UV light bulbs (which look similar to ordinary fluorescent bulbs) housed in transparent quartz sleeves. Water is irradiated by light at the ultraviolet frequency as it passes between the bulb and the sleeve.

It's important that the water coming in is relatively clean — the dirtier the water, the less effective UV disinfection will be. The quartz sleeves should be cleaned periodically, and the bulbs will need replacing two to three times a year.

The capital cost for a system is £200, and replacement bulbs are roughly £18.

Conclusions

According to a 1992 MORI survey, one third of consumers are not satisfied with the safety or the quality of their tap water. In fact the standards of UK drinking water are very high. Currently most tap water meets these standards. So there is no need to panic about the quality of your water. The health risks you incur from drinking water are minimal compared to smoking, driving a car, breathing urban air, or even eating food. (The one contaminant you should be concerned about is lead, and the best way to deal with it is by replacing any lead plumbing in your house.)

In general, unless you're unhappy with the taste of your tap water, or there are specific contaminants in your water that you want to remove, expensive home filtering systems are probably not worth the money.

Bottled water, too, is not worth the expense — unless you prefer the taste.

However, it is worth being concerned about water in a wider sense. Water is essential to us and to all other living creatures. It is dangerous and short-sighted to pollute waterways and to deplete water supplies. What is needed is a two-pronged approach to preserve our water resources: good pollution control and integrated demand management.

When it comes to water pollution, the best approach is prevention. This means that you should avoid putting solvents, paints, oil, chemicals and other unsuitable substances down the drain. Prevention is particularly important when it comes to groundwater, because it is so difficult to clean up groundwater once it is polluted. This means strict legislation backed up by strict monitoring and enforcement; more control of pollution at source; and changes to modern farming practices to prevent nitrate and pesticide pollution entering watercourses.

As drinking water standards become stricter, the cost of providing it increases. In the final analysis then, is our water safe to drink? The answer is yes, but that doesn't mean we can take it for granted.

If global warming trends continue, we could be looking at long-term changes in rainfall that will result in shrinking water supplies. This means water will become more valuable and less readily available: two powerful incentives to use less.

The water suppliers need to invest more money in infrastructure — ensuring that more than a mere three quarters of the expensively treated water gets to the consumer. It is the duty of Government to set mandatory standards on leaks for the industry. Consumers should not be penalised by companies or statutory suppliers for faults of management. And the supply companies in England and Wales must remember their first duty should be to the customer, not their shareholders. The level of complaints to the companies by the public is far too high.

We all have responsibility for the quality of our water, Government, industry, water suppliers as well as you and I.

Glossary

Abstraction
The removal of water from surface or groundwater sources for domestic, commercial or industrial use.

Acidic
Having a pH value less than 7.

Adsorption
The process by which one substance is taken onto the surface of another substance by physical and/or chemical forces.

Aeration
The exposure of water to air, so that air becomes dissolved in the water.

Alkalinity
The ability of a water solution to neutralise an acid.

Amoebic Dysentery
Inflammation of the intestine caused by a strain of amoeba. Characterised by severe diarrhoea containing blood and mucus.

Aquifer
An underground formation of porous, water-bearing rock, sand or gravel.

Bacillary Dysentery
Inflammation of the intestine caused by a strain of bacteria. Characterised by severe diarrhoea containing blood and mucus.

Basic
(see pH) Capable of combining with an acid in water to form a salt, and hydroxide ions; very basic water is not palatable.

Carcinogenic
Having the ability to cause cancer.

Catchment
Any surface area that collects run-off during a fall of rain; the area from which individual rivers, lakes or reservoirs collect water.

Cholera
Disease of the small intestine characterised by severe vomiting and diarrhoea. Caused by a strain of bacterium. Often fatal.

Coagulation
A process in which a coagulant (typically aluminium sulphate) is added to water, causing suspended material to group together into aggregate 'flocs' which are subsequently settled out by sedimentation and/or filtration. Used to remove turbidity and colour.

Colloid
A substance consisting of ultramicroscopic particles, usually viscous or gelatinous.

Contaminant
Any undesirable physical, chemical or microbiological substance in water.

Cryptosporidium
A gastroenteritis causing protozoan, which survives in water supplies in the form of oocysts. Symptoms can last for two weeks. It is a major cause of death amongst AIDS sufferers and others with suppressed immune response systems. Boiling the water kills it.

Derogation
Water companies can apply for permission to lower standards, for a specific period of time for a specific aspect of water quality, below the level dictated by the law. These permits are called derogations but are not permitted for toxic substances. If you ask your supplier to send you a list of what's in your tap water, then the more derogations you see on the list, the less safe it may be.

Disinfection
The removal, destruction or inactivation of pathogens in water.

Effluent
The liquid waste from industrial, agricultural or sewage plant outlets.

Epidemiological Data
Data obtained from studying how frequent a particular disease or condition is and how it is distributed in the population.

Faecal
To do with waste matter discharged from the bowels.

Faecal coliform bacteria
A group of bacteria found in vast numbers in human and animal faeces. Since their presence in water indicates potential faecal contamination, they are considered 'indicator species'.

Filtration
The process of passing water through the pores of a filter to remove suspended particles.

Giardia
A dangerous organism found in contaminated water supplies, particularly if contaminated by sewage. Symptoms develop one to four weeks after ingestion and include explosive, watery, foul-smelling diarrhoea, gas in the stomach, nausea and loss of appetite. Boiling water for 20 minutes will kill the cysts.

Groundwater
Water held in water-bearing rocks beneath the surface of the earth.

Hardness
A property of water caused by dissolved calcium and magnesium salts. Hard waters cause scale formation in pipes and kettles. Soft water is created by the presence of carbonate and bi-carbonate; it is often acidic and corrosive.

Indicator species
As it is difficult and expensive to screen water samples for all possible pathogens, one species (usually faecal coliform bacteria) are used as indicators of faecal contamination and therefore the possible presence of pathogens.

Infectious hepatitis
Disease of the liver.

Ion
An atom or molecule that has lost one or more electrons to become a positively charged cation, or has gained one or more electrons to become a negatively charged anion.

Leaching
The process by which substances are removed from a solid mass by the action of a percolating liquid and are carried away in solution or suspension.

Oocyst
The dormant form of a protozoan parasite such as Cryptosporidium.

Pathogen
An organism that causes disease.

Peak demand
The maximum demand (e.g. for water) during a particular period of time, e.g.. daily or annually.

pH
A logarithmic measure of the acidity or alkalinity of water. A pH of 7 is neutral, a pH of less than 7 is acidic, and a pH of more than 7 is alkaline.

Poliomyelitis
A viral disease that affects the central nervous system, often causing paralysis.

Potable
Safe to drink; free from disease-causing organisms and toxic substances.

Protozoan
Microscopic one-celled creatures like amœbae which are members of the subkingdom Protozoa.

Raw water
Another term for untreated water.

Run-off
Water derived from snow or rain that flows across the surface of land into streams, rivers and lakes.

Schistosomiasis
A chronic tropical disease caused by flatworm infestations in the blood vessels of the pelvic region.

Sedimentation
A process for removing suspended solids by passing water slowly through a tank, allowing sediments to settle out through the force of gravity.

Surface water
Bodies of water on the surface of the Earth: e.g. streams, rivers, ponds, lakes, oceans.

Suspended solids
Particles of grit, sand or organic material floating (suspending) in a body of water.

Toxicological data
Data based on (usually animal) studies of how poisonous a particular substance is.

Turbidity
A measure of the amount of particulate matter present in water. An optical property of water resulting from the scattering of light by suspended and colloidal particles.

Typhoid
A bacterial disease characterised by fever, intestinal irritation and a rash on the chest and abdomen.

UV
Ultraviolet light, which has a frequency just beyond the violet end of the visible spectrum, has disinfectant properties and is used to kill organisms in contaminated water.

Water soluble
Having the ability to dissolve in water.

Water table
The level underground beneath which the rocks are saturated with groundwater.

UK standards for drinking water

The following is the list of parameters established by the 1989 Water Supply (Water Quality) Regulations. Some technical details have been omitted. Unless otherwise specified, prescribed concentration values are maximum values.

Substance	Prescribed Concentration Value	Units of Measurement
Organoleptic		
Colour	20	mg/l Pt/Co scale
Turbidity	4	Formazin turbidity units
Odour at 25°C	3	dilution no.
Taste at 25°C	3	dilution no.
Physico-Chemical		
Temperature	25	°C
Hydrogen Ion	9.5	pH unit
Conductivity at 20°C	1500	uS/cm
Chloride	400	mg/l
Sulphates	250	mg/l
Calcium	250	mg/l
Magnesium	50	mg/l
Sodium	150	mg/l
Potassium	12	mg/l

Aluminium	200 ug/l
Dry Residues	1500 mg/l after drying @180
Total Hardness	60 (min.) mg/l
Alkalinity	30 (min.) ug HCO3/l

Substances Undesirable in Excessive Amounts

Nitrates	50 mg/l
Nitrites	0.1 mg/l
Ammonium	0.5 mg/l
Kjeldahl Nitrogen	1 mg/l
Oxidizability	5 mg/l
	(potassium permanganate)
Total Organic Carbon	no significant increase over
	that normally observed
Hydrogen Sulphide	not detectable
Dissolved or Emulsified	10 ug/l
Hydrocarbons	
Phenols	0.5 ug/l
Surfactants	200 ug/l
Iron	200 ug/l
Manganese	50 ug/l
Copper	3000 ug/l
Zinc	5000 ug/l
Phosphorus	2200 ug/l
Fluoride	1500 ug/l
Silver	10 ug/l
Trihalomethanes	100 ug/l

Toxic Substances

Arsenic	50 ug/l
Cadmium	5 ug/l
Cyanides	50 ug/l
Chromium	50 ug/l
Mercury	1 ug/l
Nickel	50 ug/l
Lead	50 ug/l
Antimony	10 ug/l
Selenium	10 ug/l

Pesticides — Individual	0.1 ug/l
Pesticides — Total	0.5 ug/l
Polycyclic Aromatic Hydrocarbons	0.2 ug/l

Microbiological

Total Coliforms	0 100 ml
Faecal Coliforms	0 100 ml
Faecal Streptococci	0 100 ml
Sulphite Reducing Clostridia	0 20 ml
Colony counts	no significant increase over that normally observed

Resource Guide

This lists organisations, consultants, equipment suppliers and publications concerned with the issues described in this book.

The inclusion of any company does not constitute a recommendation for that company's products or services. Potential customers are advised to contact several companies to compare products, services and prices.

Many publications and products products listed can be ordered from the Centre for Alternative Technology Mail Order Service either by post with a cheque or on the credit card 24 hour answerphone line, 01654 703409. Postage and packing rates: goods total below £10 add 20% (min. £1); total £10-£15 add £3.00; total £15-£40 add £4.00; total over £40 add £4.50; overseas orders add 30% (minimum £1.95).

This guide is ordered as follows:

General Organisations
  Customer service committees

Conservation of water

Consultancy

Descaling

Infrastructure

Pumps

Quality testing

Resource evaluation

Treatment and purification

Publications - available from C.A.T. and elsewhere

General Organisations

BRITISH WATER
1 Queen Anne's Gate, London SW1H 9BT.
Tel. 0171 957 4554   Fax. 0171 957 4565.
Water industry trade association incorporating British Effluent and Water Association, and British Water Industries Group (BWIG). Represents 400 companies involved in all aspects of the water cycle.

CENTRE FOR ALTERNATIVE TECHNOLOGY
Machynlleth, Powys SY20 9AZ.
Tel. 01654 702400   Fax. 01654 702782.
The Centre has over 20 years experience of running its own independent water supply, using a slow sand filter and ultraviolet (UV) treatment. Information, publications, consultancy service and residential courses available.

CHARTERED INSTITUTION OF WATER AND ENVIRONMENTAL MANAGEMENT

15 John Street, London WC1N 2EB.
Tel. 0171 831 3110 Fax. 0171 405 4967.
Trade body for water and environmental management, offers professional qualifications, structured training, journals newsletters and technical publications.

DEPARTMENT OF THE ENVIRONMENT NORTHERN IRELAND (ENVIRONMENTAL PROTECTION)

Calvert Ho., 23 Castle Place, Belfast BT1 1FY.
Tel. 01232 254754 Fax. 01232 254700.
Aims to maintain and develop water and sewerage services to required quality and environmental standards to Northern Ireland. Legislative/ regulatory function. Provides standard information pack.

DEPARTMENT OF THE ENVIRONMENT NORTHERN IRELAND (WATER SERVICE)

Head Office, North Land House,
3 Frederick Street, Belfast BT1 2NR.
Tel. 01232 244711 Fax. 01232 354888.
Aims to ensure that wholesome drinking water is supplied in Northern Ireland.

DEPARTMENT OF THE ENVIRONMENT (WATER DIRECTORATE)

Romney Ho., 43 Marsham St., London SW1P 3PY.
Tel. 0171 276 8808 Fax. 0171 276 8405.
Ensures that the water companies in England and Wales provide a wholesome supply of drinking water and meet the requirements of the water quality regulations.

DRINKING WATER INSPECTORATE

Romney Ho., 43 Marsham St., London SW1P 3PY.
Tel. 0171 276 8808/8666 Fax. 0171 276 8405.
Oversees that water companies supply water that is safe to drink and meets standards set in Water Supply (Water Quality) Regulations.

ENVIRONMENT AGENCY

Rivers House, Waterside Drive, Aztec West, Almondsbury, Avon BS12 4UD.
Tel. 01454 624400 Fax. 01454 624409.
(Emergency hotline. 0800 807060)
Organisation resulting from the merger of the National Rivers Authority, the Waste Regulation Authorities, Her Majesty's Inspectorate of Pollution and several smaller units from the Department of the Environment. Aims to provide a comprehensive approach to the protection and management of the environment by combining the regulation of land, air and water. Covers England and Wales.

ENVIRONMENT HERITAGE SERVICE

Calvert House, 23 Castle Place, Belfast, Northern Ireland BT1 1FY.
Tel. 01232 254754 Fax. 01232 254700.
Aims to maintain and develop water and sewerage services to required quality and environmental standards, to Northern Ireland. Offers publications such as factsheets, brochures and research reports.

ENVIRONMENTAL INDUSTRIES COMMISSION Ltd.

6 Donaldson Road, London NW6 6NB.
Tel. 0171 624 2728 Fax. 0171 328 5910.
A trade association lobbying for U.K. and E.C. Government support for environmental technology and services industry. Aims to promote awareness of the commercial and environmental technologies and services, and to organise education programme targeting mainstream industry to promote the use of environmental technologies and services.

FRIENDS OF THE EARTH

26-28 Underwood Street, London N1 7JQ.
Tel. 0171 490 1555 Fax. 0171 490 0881.
Campaigning to maintain and enhance the quality of water. Excellent free briefing sheets on water privatisation, nitrates and drinking water.

INDUSTRIAL WATER SOCIETY

Mill House, Tolson's Mill, Lichfield Street, Fazeley, Tamworth B78 3QB.
Tel. 01827 289558 Fax. 01827 250408.
Promotes information and research about industrial and commercial water use. Publication 'Waterline'.

INSTITUTE OF HYDROLOGY

Maclean Building, Crowmarsh Gifford, Wallingford OX10 8BB.
Tel. 01491 838800 Fax. 01491 692424.
Carries out studies of water, including

water resources and water quality.
Reference library available to visitors

INSTITUTE OF PLUMBING
64 Station Lane, Hornchurch, Essex RM12 6NB
Tel. 01708 472 791 Fax. 01708 448987

INSTITUTION OF WATER OFFICERS
Heriot House, 12 Summerhill Terrace, Newcastle-upon-Tyne NE4 6EB.
Tel. 0191 230 5150 Fax. 0191 230 2880.
Technical feature articles, Institution news and reports and articles of a general interest for senior management and engineers within the water and waste industries.

INTERMEDIATE TECHNOLOGY DEVELOPMENT GROUP
Myson House, Railway Terrace, Rugby, Warwickshire CV21 3HT.
Tel. 01788 560631 Fax. 01788 540270.
Covers information on water supply, resources, rainwater, treatment and training. Library and publications.

INTERNATIONAL ASSOCIATION ON WATER QUALITY
1 Queen Anne's Gate, London SW1H 9BT.
Tel. 0171 222 3848 Fax. 0171 233 1197.
Water pollution control worldwide. Membership includes access to integrated communications network of publications, conferences, and specialist groups.

INTERNATIONAL SOCIETY FOR THE PREVENTION OF WATER POLLUTION
Little Orchard, Bentworth, Alton, Hants. GU34 5RB.
Tel. 01420 56225 Fax. on request.
Charity investigating water pollution problems, seas, lakes, rivers, streams, etc. Holds technical information.

LABORATORY OF THE GOVERNMENT CHEMIST
Queens Rd., Teddington, Middlesex TW11 0LY.
Tel. 0181 943 7000 Fax. 0181 943 2767.
Referee in prosecutions under legislation relating to trade description, revenue protection and human health.

LIVE WATER TRUST
Hawkwood College, Painswick Old Road, Stroud, Glos. GL6 7QW.
Tel. 01452 812503 Fax. 01452 525667.

Researches and promotes an understanding of the life-giving quality of water.

NATIONAL ANTI-FLUORIDATION CAMPAIGN
36 Station Road, Thames Ditton, Surrey KT7 0NS.
Tel. 0181 398 2117 Fax. None.
Voluntary body fighting for the end of fluoridation of all public water in the UK and N.Ireland.

NATIONAL CONSUMER COUNCIL
20 Grosvenor Gardens, London SW1W 0DH.
Tel. 0171 730 3469 Fax. 0171 730 0191.
Consumer 'watchdog' - research and policy organisation for disadvantaged consumers.

NATIONAL PURE WATER ASSOCIATION
17 Sycamore Lane, West Bretton, Wakefield, W. Yorks. WF4 4JR.
Tel/Fax. 01924 830097.
Voluntary organisation, tap water pollution - has books on fluoridation lead in water, etc.

NATURAL MINERAL WATER ASSOCIATION
20 - 22 Stakely Street, London WC2B 5LR.
Tel. 0171 430 0356 Fax. 0171 831 6014.
Trade association for mineral water suppliers.

OFFICE OF WATER SERVICES
Centre City Tower, 7 Hill Street, Birmingham B5 4UA.
Tel. 0121 625 1300 Fax. 0121 625 1400.
Government department responsible for ensuring water industry provides quality/efficient service. Provides information service, leaflets, publications. Will provide information on regional offices.

SCOTTISH ENVIRONMENTAL PROTECTION AGENCY
1 South Street, Perth, Scotland PH2 8NJ.
Tel. 01738 627989 Fax. 01738 630997.
Government body that aims to provide a comprehensive approach to the protection and management of the environment of Scotland.

WATER AID

Prince Consort House, 27-29 Albert Embankment, London SE1 7UB.
Tel. 0171 793 4500   Fax. 0171 793 4545.
Charitable organisation focussing on self-help, low cost water schemes for sustainable development, providing clean, safe water for domestic and agricultural purposes.

WATER COMPANIES ASSOCIATION

1 Queen Anne's Gate, London SW1H 9BT.
Tel. 0171 222 0644   Fax. 0171 222 3366.
The Association is the national representative body for the only supply companies which provide water to 25% of the population of England and Wales. The objectives of the Association are to represent, promote and protect the common interests of its members and provide a forum within which members can discuss matters of mutual interest and concern. (The water supply companies were established in the private sector many years ago but were brought within a new water industry system of economic, product and service regulation by the Water Act 1989)

WATER DYNAMICS Ltd.

1a New Street, Mawdesley, Omskirk, Lancs' L40 2ON
Tel. 0170 482 2615   Fax. 0170 482 2615.
Supplies complete systems for greywater management, saving up to 30% of water consumed.

WATER SERVICES ASSOCIATION

1 Queen Anne's Gate, London SW1H 9BT.
Tel. 0171 957 4567   Fax. 0171 957 4666.
Association of the 10 water and sewage undertakers in England and Wales. Promotes interests of these, provides information and fora for discussion.

WATER TRAINING INTERNATIONAL

Tadley Court, Tadley Common Road, Tadley, Nr. Basingstoke, RG26 3TB.
Tel. 01734 813011   Fax. 01734 817000.
Provides training courses in all aspects of water management and technology. Consultancy service provided.

Customer Service Committees

Each region in England and Wales has its own CSC set up by Ofwat to mediate between the water and sewerage companies and customers. There are ten. The telephone numbers identified by * are charged at the local rate.

OFFICE OF WATER SERVICES

(See above)

OFWAT CENTRAL CSC

1st Floor, 77 Paradise Circus Queensway, Birmingham B1 2DZ.
Tel. 0121 212 5202 (0345 023953)*
Office hours: 8.45 am - 4.45 pm.
Responsible for customers of: Severn Trent Water Ltd., South Staffordshire Water plc.

OFWAT EASTERN CSC

Ground Floor, Carlyle House, Carlyle Road, Cambridge CD4 3DN.
Tel. 01223 323889 (0345 959369)*
Office hours: 9.00 am - 5.00 pm.
Responsible for customers of: Anglian Water Services Ltd., Cambridge Water Company, Essex and Suffolk Water plc. Tendring Hundred Water Services Ltd.

OFWAT NORTHUMBRIA CSC

2nd Floor, 35 Nelson Street, Newcastle-upon-Tyne NEl SAN.
Tel. 0191 221 0646 (0345 089367)*
Office hours: 8.30 am - 5.00 pm Mon-Thurs, 8.30 am - 4.30 pm Fri. Responsible for customers of: Northumbrian Water Ltd., North East Water plc. Hartlepool Water plc.

OFWAT NORTH WEST CSC

Suite 902, 9th Floor, Bridgewater House, Whitworth St., Manchester Ml 6LT.
Tel. 0161 236 6112 (0345 056316)*
Office hours: 9.00 am - 5.00 pm.
Responsible for customers of North West Water Ltd.

OFWAT SOUTHERN CSC

3rd Floor, 15-17 Ridgmount Street, London WC1E 7AH.
Tel. 0171 636 3656 (0345 581658)*
Office hours: 9.00 am 5.30 pm Mon-Thurs, 9.00 am - 5.15 pm Fri. Responsible for customers of: Southern Water Services Ltd., Portsmouth Water plc. South East Water Ltd., Mid-Kent Water plc.

Folkestone & Dover Water Services Ltd.

OFWAT CSC FOR THE SOUTH WEST
1st Floor, Broadwalk House,
Southernhay West, Exeter EX1 1TS.
Tel. 01392 428028 (0345 959059)*
Office hours: 8.45 am - 4.45 pm.
Responsible for customers of: South West
Water Services Ltd.

OFWAT THAMES CSC
2nd Floor 15-17 Ridgmount Street,
London WC1 E 7AH.
Tel.0171 636 3656 (0345 581658)*
Office hours: 9.00 am - 5.30 pm Mon-
Thurs, 9.00 am - 5.15 pm Fri. Responsible
for customers of: Thames Water Utilities
Ltd., Three Valleys Water plc. East Surrey
Water plc. North Surrey Water Ltd., Mid-
Southern Water plc. Sutton District Water
plc.

OFWAT CSC FOR WALES
Room 140, Caradog House, 1-6 St Andrews
Place, Cardiff CF1 3BE.
Tel. 01222 239852 (0345 078267)*
Office hours: 8.30 am - 4.30 pm.
Responsible for customers of: Dwr Cymru
Cyfyngedig, Chester Waterworks
Company, Wrexham and East
Denbighshire Water Company.

OFWAT WESSEX CSC
Unit 2, The Hide Market, West St,
St. Phillips, Bristol BS2 0BH.
Tel. 0117 955 7001 (0345 078268)*
Office hours: 8.45 am - 4.45 pm.
Responsible for customers of: Wessex
Water Services Ltd., Bournemouth and
West Hampshire Water plc. Bristol Water
plc. Cholderton & District Water
Company Ltd.

OFWAT YORKSHIRE CSC
Symons House, Belgrave Street,
Leeds LS2 8DF.
Tel. 0113 234 0874 (0345 089368)*
Office hours: 8.30 am - 5.00 pm.
Responsible for customers of: Yorkshire
Water Services Ltd., York Waterworks plc.

WATER SERVICES ASSOCIATION
(See above)

Conservation of Water

AC DEVELOPMENTS Ltd.
Braughing Friars, Braughing,
Hertfordshire SG11 2NS.
Tel. 01279 771100 Fax. 01279 771111.
Manufactures rain water saving device
'Rain Saver', an automatic butt filler and
overflow device.

ACTION EUROPE Ltd.
Business & Technology Centre, Bessemer
Drive, Stevenage, Herts. SG1 2DX.
Tel. 01438 310189 Fax. 01483 310182.
Supplies 'Platypus' water and energy
conservation system for showers and taps.

AIRSTREAM PRODUCTS Ltd.
Airstream House, Brook Street,
Cheadle, Cheshire SK8 2BN.
Tel. 0161 428 7544 Fax. 0161 428 7135.
Water control systems.

CHESS INDUSTRIES plc
Central Chambers, London Road,
Alderley Edge, Cheshire SK9 7DZ.
Tel. 01625 585565 Fax. 01625 585584.
Supplies 'SmartFlush' urinal control
system. Provides consultancy service on
water conservation.

DART VALLEY SERVICES
Cliff Works, 59 Roundham Road,
Paignton, Devon TQ4 6DS.
Tel. 01803 529021 Fax. 01803 559016.
Energy control and conservation within
the plumbing sector.

EX-OR Ltd.
Haydock La., Haydock, Merseyside WA11
9UJ.
Tel. 01942 719229 Fax. 01942 272767.
Supplies automatic water and lighting
controls.

**FLOW CONTROL WATER CONSER-
VATION Ltd.**
Nat West Bank Buildings, 89 Brighton Street,
Wallasey, Merseyside L44 6QJ.
Tel. 0151 638 8811 Fax. 0151 638 4137.
Manufactures water-saving devices
including some for urinals.

FREEWATER UK Ltd.
Peak House, Shepley Lane,
Marple, Cheshire SK6 7JW.
Tel. 0161 449 7220/1 Fax. 0161 449 7242.

Franchise company offering systems for grey and rain water recycling.

FULLFLOW SYSTEMS Ltd.
Fullflow House, Holbrook Avenue, Holbrook, Sheffield S19 5FF.
Tel. 0114 247 3655 Fax. 0114 247 7805.
Designs, supplies and installs rainwater systems - syphonic roof drainage system and gutter and rainwater systems.

GLOBEMALL Ltd.
1 Woodbridge Road, Ipswich IP4 2EA.
Tel. 01473 259232 Fax. 01473 286285.
Supplies and installs waterless urinals.

GREEN SHOP
Bisley, Stroud, Gloucestershire GL6 7BX.
Tel/Fax. 01452 770629.
Has a catalogue of environmentally and ethically aware products. Supplies 'Wisy-Filter collectors': filters and collects rain water. Provides water for the toilet, washing machine, household cleaning, the garden, etc.

HYDREC
Woodside House, 7 Woodside Green, London SE25 5EY.
Tel. 0181 655 1696 Fax. 0181 654 8302.
Manufactures and installs domestic grey water systems

MEP CONTROLS
Hill House, 36 Rayne Road, Braintree, Essex CM7 7QP.
Tel. 01376 323122 Fax. 01376 323109.
Supplies 'Aqualite' water management system, to save water and lighting costs in public or workplace toilets.

PRACTICAL ALTERNATIVES
Tir Gaia Solar Village, Rhayader LD6 5DY.
Tel/Fax. 01597 810929.
Develops and markets resource-saving products geared to domestic situations, specifically water-saving sewage systems.

PREMIERE plc
The Rise, Stow Road, Purleigh, Chelmsford, Essex CM3 6RR.
Tel. 01621 829600 Fax. 01621 829700.
Supplies the 'Pressure Butt', a device for allowing capture of rain water and re-use of grey water for the garden and/or for flushing toilets. Approved by the Water Research Council.

RAIN DRAIN Ltd.
Albert Mills, Mill Street West, Dewsbury, West Yorkshire WF12 9AE.
Tel. 01924 455804 Fax. 01924 465925.
Manufactures and distributes RAIN-SAVA kit which allows the diversion of rainwater from roof downpipes and to use or store the water.

THERMO SPEED
20 Kansas Avenue, Salford, Greater Manchester M5 2GL.
Tel. 0161 872 0426 Fax. 0161 848 7273.
Off the shelf range of industrial sensors, controls and instrumentation.

WATER MANAGEMENT SYSTEMS (UK)
Suite 6-7, Robin Ent. Centre, Leeds Road, Idle, W. Yorks. BD10 9TE.
Tel. 01274 611131 Fax. 01274 611132.
Offers packages to companies including water cost control, leak detection, installation and treatment. Supplies urinal flush controller. Full consultancy service nationwide.

Consultancy

ACER ENVIRONMENTAL CONSULTANTS Ltd.
Acer House, Brooklands, 680 Budshead Road, Plymouth PL6 5XR.
Tel. 01752 769675 Fax. 01752 769677.
Acer Environmental is a specialist environmental consultancy, laboratory and scientific services company, operating worldwide. Specialises in water and environmental management, land development, analytical testing, policy statements, environmental audits and risk assessment. Part of the Acer Group of companies, owned by Welsh Water plc.

ACER GROUP Ltd.
Plymouth House, Plymouth Road, Penarth, South Glamorgan CF6 2YF.
Tel. 01222 704321 Fax. 01222 709793.
International consultancy covering civil, structural and environmental engineering, water supply, water treatment works, sewerage/sewage treatment, EIA.

CHESS INDUSTRIES plc
(See Conservation of Water)

HEPWORTH MINERALS AND CHEMICALS Ltd.
Brookside Hall, Congleton Road, Sandbach, Cheshire CW11 0TR.
Tel. 01270 752752 Fax. 01270 752753.
Supplier of high quality filter sands and produces specialist resins with associated products. Consultancy provided.

HYDRO-LOGIC Ltd.
Old Grammar School, Church Street, Bromyard, Herefordshire HR7 4DP.
Tel. 01885 483789 Fax. 01885 483 792.
Specialises in water resource management. Has a range of monitoring services for water flows, water quality and effluent discharges.

MACHINE CONSERVATION
Jim Barr, 34 The Ridgeway, Flitwick, Bedford MK45 1DH.
Tel. 01525 712824 Fax. None.
Consultant, smallscale (less than 1m diam) windpumps.

MEMCOR Ltd.
Wirksworth, Derbyshire DE4 4BG.
Tel. 01629 823811 Fax. 01629 825169.
Designs, manufactures, installs and commissions complete separation and purification systems.

WATER MANAGEMENT CONSULTANTS Ltd.
2/3 Wyle Cop, Shrewsbury SY1 1UT.
Tel. 01743 231793 Fax. 01743 232894.
Specialises in groundwater resource evaluation and provision of integrated water services to mining industry.

WATER MANAGEMENT SYSTEMS (UK)
(See Conservation of Water)

WATER RESEARCH CENTRE plc
Henley Road, Medmenham, Marlow, Buckinghamshire SL7 2HD.
Tel. 01491 571531 Fax. 01491 579094.
R&D within the water industry. Covers aspects of water research technology and innovation. Offers advisory and consulting services.

WATER TRAINING INTERNATIONAL
(See General Organisations)

Descaling

CLEAN FUTURE INTERNATIONAL Ltd.
101A Petherton Road, London N5 2QT.
Tel. 0171 359 5155 Fax. 0171 359 5680.
Designs manufactures and supplies descalers for hard water for domestic and commercial use.

ETCETERA(UK) Ltd.
Funtley Court, Funtley Hill, Fareham, Hants. PO16 7UY.
Tel. 01329 231975 Fax. 01329 220657.
Developed 'Enigma', an electronic device to remove and prevent scale build-up in hard-water systems without the use of water softeners or chemicals. Applied by wrapping a signal cable around the pipe to be treated.

TACOTHERM LAMACO Ltd.
28 Bristol Gardens, London W9 2JQ.
Tel. 0171 266 4528 Fax. 0171 266 4524.
Offers an electronic descaling system for commercial and industrial applications saving costs on maintenance, downtime, and chemicals. Can prevent scaling and remove existing deposits within pipes without chemicals.

Infrastructure

B&B(GRP) MOULDINGS
PO Box 202, Wadhurst, East Sussex TN5 7NG.
Tel. 01797 224088 Fax. 01797 224086.
Glassfibre access and chamber covers suitable for installation in water and sewerage schemes. Currently used by many Water Authorities.

FRANKLIN HODGE INDUSTRIES Ltd.
Ramsden Road, Rotherwas Industrial Estate, Hereford HR2 6LR.
Tel. 01432 269605 Fax. 01432 277454.
Liquid storage tanks worldwide.

HEPWORTH INDUSTRIAL PLASTICS
Hazlehead, Stocksbridge, Sheffield S30 5HG.
Tel. 01226 370510 Fax. 01226 762850.
Pipe manufacturer.

Pumps

ABACHEM ENGINEERING Ltd.
Jessop Way, Newark, Notts. NG24 2ER.
Tel. 01636 76483 Fax. 01636 708632.
Siphon pumps for surface water or to a depth up to 7.5m and bore hole pumps to a depth of 150m.

ALLSPEEDS
PO Box 43, Royal Works,
Atlas Street, Accrington BB5 5LP.
Tel. 01254 235441 Fax. 01254 382899.
Manufactures and supplies hydraulic ram pumps.

CLAYTON EXPRESS
Fishergreen, Ripon, North Yorkshire HG4 1NL.
Tel. 01765 690906/604606
Fax. (mobile) 0860 913628.
Manufactures hand pumps for shallow and deep wells.

CONSALLEN GROUP
23 Oakwood Hill Industrial Est.,
Loughton, Essex IG10 3TZ.
Tel/Fax. 01787 248535.
Manufacturer of hand pumps and bore-hole drilling rigs.

GREEN & CARTER
Vulcan Works, Ashbrittle,
Wellington, Somerset TA21 0LQ.
Tel. 01823 672365 Fax. 01823 672950.
Manufacturer of high duty hydraulic rams.

GRUNDFOS PUMPS Ltd.
Grovebury Road, Leighton Buzzard,
Bedfordshire LU7 8TL.
Tel. 01525 850000 Fax. 01525 850011.
Manufactures various pumps.

INGERSOLL-DRESSER PUMPS
PO Box 17, Lowfield Work, Newark,
Nottinghamshire NG24 3EN.
Tel. 01636 705151 Fax. 01636 705991.
Manufactures, sells and installs pumps and pumping equipment.

LDH INTERNATIONAL
The Levels, Astley, Shrewsbury,
Shropshire SY4 4BY.
Tel. 01939 250777 Fax. 01939 250213.
Supplies a range of pumps including submersible pumps.

LVM Ltd.
Aerogen House, Old Oak Close,
Arlesey, Beds. SG15 6XD.
Tel. 01462 733336 Fax. 01462 730466.
Supplies low voltage d.c. products, including pumps.

MACHINE CONSERVATION
(See Consultancy)

MID WALES WELDED PRODUCTS Ltd.
Westgate St, Llanidloes, Powys SY18 6HN.
Tel. 01686 412104 Fax. 01686 413673.
Supplies new and refurbished wind pumps and parts.

MONO PUMPS Ltd.
Arnsield Works, Martin Street,
Audenshaw, Manchester M34 5DQ.
Tel. 0161 339 9000 Fax. 0161 344 0727.
Manufacturer and supplier of various pumps including borehole pumps.

SARLIN Ltd.
Pumps Division, Highcliffe Road, Hamilton Industrial Park, Leicester LE5 1TY.
Tel. 0116 246 1527 Fax. 0116 246 0813.
Pumps (submersible and free standing) from 2kW - 450kW.

SMEDEGAARD PUMPS
Unit 7, Barhams Close, Wylds Road,
Bridgewater, Somerset TA6 4DS.
Tel. 01278 458686 Fax. 01278 452454.
Supplies a range of pumps for domestic and commercial installations.

SPP Ltd.
Theale Cross, Calcot, Reading, Berks. RG31 7SP.
Tel. 01734 323123 Fax. 01734 323302.
Manufacturer of pumping equipment.

STUART TURNER Ltd.
47 Market Place, Henley-on-Thames,
Oxfordshire RG9 2AD.
Tel. 01491 572655 Fax. 01491 573704.
Manufactures various pumps.

Quality testing

ROBERTSON LABORATORIES
Llanrhos, Llandudno, Gwynedd LL30 1SA.
Tel. 01492 581811   Fax. 01492 592030.
Accredited laboratory providing analytical services to the environmental sector for water, wastewater, air pollution, soil and contaminated land testing.

SEVERN TRENT LABORATORIES
Head Office, Tile Hill, Coventry CV4 9GU.
Tel. 01203 692692   Fax. 01203 856575.
Commercial laboratory providing range of analytical and scientific services to industry and local government. NAMAS accredited.

SOUTHERN SCIENCE Ltd.
Vanguard House, Churchill Court, Manor Royal, Crawley, West Sussex RH10 2PN.
Tel. 01293 538444   Fax. 01293 530830.
Subsidiary of Southern Water Group. Provides integrated laboratory water resource and environmental services.

Resource evaluation

BRITISH SOCIETY OF DOWSERS
Sycamore Barn, Hastingleigh,
Ashford, Kent TN25 5HW.
Tel/Fax. 01233 750253.
Quarterly journal, lectures and meetings on the use of dowsing for geophysical, medical, agricultural and other purposes. Books and equipment available.

WATER MANAGEMENT CONSULTANTS Ltd.
(See Consultancy)

Treatment & purification

ALDOUS & STAMP Ltd.
86-90 Avenue Road,
Beckenham, Kent BR3 4SA.
Tel. 0181 659 1833/4/5
Fax. 0181 676 9676.
Supplies and gives advice on treatment for independent water supplies. Supplies ultraviolet filters.

AQUA CURE plc
Aqua Cure House, Hall Street,
Southport, Merseyside PR9 0SE.
Tel. 01704 501616   Fax. 01704 544916.
Manufacturer of water filter systems and purifiers for domestic and industrial use.

AQUARIAN AGENCY Ltd.
38 Weir Road, Wimbledon,
London SW19 8UG.
Tel. 0181 944 5985   Fax. 0181 944 7327.
Researches and manufactures materials and products fabricated using 'Water Vortex' technology.

ARBOUR TECH Ltd.
Kingsland, Leominster,
Herefordshire HR6 9SF.
Tel. 01568 708840   Fax. 01568 708974.
Water purification by ultraviolet and/or filtering.

BERGLEN GROUP Ltd.
Masons House, Kingsbury Road,
London NW9 9NQ.
Tel. 0181 204 3434   Fax. 0181 204 6010.
Manufactures water filtration systems for domestic use.

CAMPHILL WATER
Oaklands Park, Newnham-on-Severn,
Gloucestershire GL14 4EQ.
Tel. 01594 516063   Fax. 01594 516821.
Supplies the 'Carefree' water quality improver, an in-line device for improving water by vortex or flowform technology.

CULLIGAN INTERNATIONAL
Blenheim Rd, Cressex Estate, High Wycombe,
Bucks. HP12 3RS.
Tel. 01494 436484   Fax. 01494 523833.
Manufactures, supplies and installs water conditioning and softening systems for domestic and industrial applications including swimming pools.

EVERPURE WATER FILTERS: CITMART
Lympne Ind. Pk., Hythe, Kent CT21 4LR.
Tel. 01303 262211   Fax. 01303 260057.
Supplies water filters.

FIELDWAY Ltd.
Croft Road, Crowborough,
East Sussex TN6 1DL.
Tel. 01892 655782   Fax. 01892 655792.
Distributes equipment for solar heating and for water purification

FOSPUR Ltd.
Alfreton Trading Estate,
Somercotes, Derby DE55 4LR.
Tel. 01773 604321/8 Fax. 01773 606901.
Conditioning raw water for industrial and
municipal use, for boiler and cooling
waters, for potable water and for trade
effluent and sewage treatment.

FUNDAMENTAL ENERGY COMPANY
Fieldway Limited, Croft Road, Crowborough,
East Sussex TN6 1DL.
Tel. 01892 655782 Fax. 01892 655792.
Manufactures an electronic water purifier
(the 'Self-Compensating Electronic Water
Purifier') which will convert dilute sewage
to potable water, replace chlorine in
purifying swimming pools, remove
Legionella bacteria from wet air conditioning systems. The system works by
passing a low voltage current between
two or more electrodes, causing the water
between the electrodes to receive a
quantity of charged ions whose property
kills bacteria and algae. As water flows
between the anodes, it is purified. The
ions also reduce the hardness in water
supplies.

HANOVIA Ltd.
145 Farnham Road, Slough,
Berkshire SL1 4XB.
Tel. 01753 812145 Fax. 01753 534277.
Supplies ultraviolet systems for water and
waste water purification.

HARMONOLOGY CENTRE
6 Myrtle Park, Glasgow G42 8UQ.
Tel. 0141 423 2566 Fax. 0141 423 2377.
Supplies the 'Aquator' water activating
and purifying unit; a portable and/or in-
line device for improving water by
energetic resonance and interference
technology (ERIT).

HEPWORTH MINERALS AND
CHEMICALS Ltd.
(See Consultancy)

KALSEP Ltd.
Doman Road, Yorktown Ind. Est., Camberley,
Surrey GU15 3DF.
Tel. 01276 675675 Fax. 01276 676276.

Supplies a range of compact, fully
automatic, self-cleaning fibrous depth
filtration systems.

KK WATER PURIFICATION Ltd.
Victory House, Victory Park Road,
Addlestone, Weybridge, Surrey KT15 2AX.
Tel. 01932 858170 Fax. 01932 847170.
UK distributor of Aquafine ultraviolet
liquid disinfection units. Provides
nationwide sales and service facility.

LDH INTERNATIONAL
(See Pumps)

LIFF INDUSTRIES Ltd.
Bayhall, Miln Road, Huddersfield,
West Yorkshire HD1 5EJ.
Tel. 01484 512537 Fax. 01484 513597.
Specialist in water treatment products,
including water softeners, filters, UV
disinfection units and scale inhibitors.

MALVAN GROUP Ltd.
4 Hercules House, Calleva Industrial Park,
Aldermaston, Berkshire RG7 8DN.
Tel. 01734 816588 Fax. 01734 819532.
Manufactures IMO steam boilers to
sterilise without using chemicals.

MEMCOR Ltd.
(See Consultancy)

NSA WATER TREATMENT SYSTEMS
NSA House, 39 Queen Street, Maidenhead,
Berks. SL6 1NB.
Tel. 01628 776044 Fax. 01628 70725.
Supplier of water treatment systems.

POLAR INTERNATIONAL (UK) Ltd.
Bell Lane, Syresham, Northants. NN13 5HP.
Tel. 01280 850456 Fax. 01280 850445.
Non-chemical water treatment and
advanced water treatment equipment for
industrial and domestic applications.

PUROLITE INTERNATIONAL Ltd.
Ashley House, Kershaw House, Great West
Rd., Hounslow, Middx. TW5 0BU.
Tel. 0181 570 4454 Fax. 0181 572 7726.
Supplier of products for the treatment of
both water and waste waters.

SENTINEL LABORATORIES Ltd.
Mitchell House, The Mardens, Ifield, Crawley,
W. Sussex RH11 0AQ.
Tel. 01293 526457 Fax. 01293 517870.
Supplies SentechPH and SentechTDS.

Applications: swimming pools, water treatment, pollution control, etc.

SHAKESBY & SONS Ltd.
97 Angela Rd, Horsford,
Norwich, Norfolk NR10 3HF.
Tel. 01603 262263   Fax. 01603 262161.
Supplier of filter systems for private water supplies.

SUNWATER Ltd.
44, Friar Street, Droitwich, Worcestershire
WR9 8ED.
Tel. 01905 771117   Fax. 01905 772270.
Ultraviolet disinfection of potable/process water as well as of sewage effluents.

VERTAC INDUSTRIES
Unit 16, Halcyon Court, St Margarets Way,
Huntingdon, Cambs PE18 6EB.
Tel. 01480 411185   Fax. 01480 413747.
Designer, manufacturer and supplier of water filters and softeners.

WATER MANAGEMENT SYSTEMS (UK)
(See Conservation of Water)

WORLD-WIDE WATER TECHNOLOGY Ltd.
PO Box 128, Rickmansworth,
Hertfordshire WD3 4PY.
Tel. 01923 777663   Fax. 01923 896066.
Supplies the 'Emerald' and 'Stel' water quality improvers, in-line devices for sterilising water and removing metals and all other harmful impurities, using advanced electrolytic technology ('Electrochemical Activation').

Publications available from C.A.T. Mail Order

C.A.T. Publications

Sewage Solutions   £7.95
Grant, Moodie and Weedon (1996) 160pp
A guide to the principles and technologies of ecologically sound sewage treatment, including reed beds and compost toilets. For the beginner.

Fertile Waste   £3.95.
Harper, (1994)   *32pp*

A guide to dry toilets and how to make a twin vault variety, with diagrams.

Water Conservation Tipsheet   30p
A4 2pp   Tips on saving water.

Hydraulic Ram   £0.30
A4 2pp.
A description of an elegant water-powered pump.

Making Use of Waste Water   £0.30
A4 2pp.
A guide to re-using household 'greywater'.

Other books

Ferrocement Water Tanks   £8.95
Watt, IT Publications (1978) 118pp.
A practical guide to designing and building long-life, low-cost tanks in thin, wire mesh reinforced mortar.

Groundwater Dams for Small-Scale Water Supply   £7.95
Nilsson, IT Publications (1988) 64pp.
Two types of dam are fully described. Both are inexpensive and suitable for water supply schemes in rural areas in developing countries.

Handbook of Gravity-Flow Water Systems   £9.95
Jordan, IT Publications (1984) 250pp.
Originally written for the construction of gravity-flow drinking water systems in Nepal, this book is equally applicable in other locations around the world.

Hand Pump Maintenance in the Context of Community Well Projects   £5.95
Pacey, IT Publications (1980) 44pp.
A guide to community well projects, including an overview of the different types of hand pump available.

Home Water Supply: How to find, filter, store and conserve it.   £15.99
S. Campbell, Garden Way (1993) 236pp.
An excellent book which addresses almost any question you may have regarding water in the home, including pump sizes, locating water, digging a pond, plumbing, water treatment and drought gardening.

Hydraulic Ram Pumps   £12.95
Jeffery et al, IT Publications (1992) 144pp.

Clearly illustrated, giving step-by-step instructions on designing, installing and operating water supply systems based on hydraulic ram pumps. Includes notes for those developing their own model.

Last Oasis: Facing Water Scarcity £9.95
Postel, Earthscan (1992) 240pp.
The third in Earthscan's Worldwatch Environmental Alert series, this book confronts the issues of mismanagement and profligacy in water use, arguing that the skills and knowledge needed for effective water husbandry do exist.

Manual on the Hydraulic Ram £5.95
Watt, IT Publications (1975) 38pp.
Provides details on how to make and maintain a small hydraulic ram on a suitable site. Also gives a more technical examination of ram performances and design considerations, followed by a useful bibliography.

Manual for Rural Water Supplies £29.95
Helvetas (Ed.), SKAT-ATOL (1980) 175pp.
Well-illustrated manual for rural water supply, based on the experiences acquired by Helvetas experts in Cameroon.

Rainwater Harvesting £11.95
Pacey & Cullis, IT Publications (1986) 224pp.
Aimed at rural development workers involved with water resources for domestic and agricultural purposes, this book demonstrates sustainable and appropriate designs with plans and case studies.

Sanitation Without Water £5.95
Winblad & Kilam, Macmillan (1985) 162pp.
Contains practical information on how to choose, build and operate simple latrine systems. Highly recommended.

Six Simple Pumps £7.25
Crouch, VITA (1983) 94pp.
Useful manual for schools, universities, and development projects. It describes a range of pumps that are relatively cheap and easy to build and maintain with local skills and materials, avoiding the use of fossil fuels. Excellent diagrams.

Slow Sand Filtration for Community Water Supply £29.99
Visscher, Paramasivam, Raman & Heijnen, IRC (1987) 149pp.

Presents established information on slow and sand filtration, as well as guidelines resulting from demonstration projects in developing countries.

Small-Scale Irrigation £7.95
Stern, IT Publications (1979) 176pp.
Presents the technical know-how needed for developing irrigated agriculture on a small-scale in rural areas. Clearly illustrated.

Surface Water Treatment for Communities in Developing Countries £14.95
Schultz & Okun, IT Publications (1992) 300pp.
Discusses basic considerations that need addressing when designing or building water treatment plants. Also presents a series of appropriate treatment requirements and processes for plants for use by communities in developing countries.

Toilet Papers £8.95
Van der Ryn, Ecological Design Press (1978) 127pp.
Provides an informative, inspiring and irreverent look at how people have dealt with human wastes over the centuries, and at what safe designs are available today that reduce water consumption and avert the necessity for expensive treatment systems. Includes plans for several types of dry and compost toilets, and for greywater systems.

Water Supplies for Rural Communities £5.95
Ball, IT Publications (1991) 64pp.
Presents lessons learnt by VSO and other organisations over more than 30 years of working on rural water supply projects.

Water Treatment and Sanitation £6.95
Mann & Williamson, IT Publications (1982) 96pp.
Excellent handbook for anyone involved in small-scale water supply and waste systems. Design information on wells, pipes, pumps, filters, toilets and sewage treatment.

Worth of Water £10.95
Pickford (Intro.), IT Publications (1991) 144pp.
A series of short, highly illuminating introductions to many of the main technologies and processes in the field of village and community level water and sanitation, ranging from household water storage to

the use of public standposts.

The following are **not** available from C.A.T.

Intermediate Technology Publications, the publishing arm of the Intermediate Technology Development Group, produces a comprehensive mail-order catalogue, **Books by Post.** It includes many publications on water supply and treatment and is obtainable from:
IT Publications, 103-105 Southampton Row, London WC1B 4HH.
Tel: 0171 436 9761   Fax: 0171 436 2013
E-mail: itpubs@gn.apc.org

Catchment and Storage of Rainwater £6.90
Pieck, Tool (1985) 52pp.
Details methods for catchment and storage of rainwater and small-scale provisions for potable water, which can be made with locally available techniques and materials.

The Dammed   **£18.00**
Pearce, Bodely Head (1992) 376pp.
A shattering statement of our continuing abuse of the world's great rivers.

Dams and the Environment   **£15.30**
Dixon, Talbot & Le Moigne, World Bank (1989) 64pp.
Reviews the environmental factors associated with large storage dam projects and the economic analysis of environmental effects.

Desalination and Water Reuse   **£178.00**
Morris (ed.), Taylor & Francis (1991) 1778pp.
Published in four volumes, this contains 131 papers from the 5th World Congress and 12th European Symposium, Malta.

Down the Drain   **£5.99**
Gordon, Macdonald (1989) 194pp.
A scathing view of current use and abuse of water, covering water pollution, water politics, water treatment and the history of water use.

Drinking Water Quality   **£19.95**
Gray, Wiley (1994) 315pp.
An unrivalled and clear guide to the

structure, regulation and operation of the water supply industry. Includes sections on: conservation, treatment and distribution, plus alternatives to mains water.

Environmentally-Sound Water Management   **£13.95**
Thanh & Biswas (eds.), OUP (1990) 276pp.

European Water: Meeting the Supply Challenges
McCann & Appleton, (1993) 106pp
A lucid and readable *Financial Times* report on groundwater pollution and over-abstraction in the EC.

The Good Water Guide: The World's Best Bottled Waters £8.95
Green, (1994) 200pp.
Lists almost 200 bottled waters from 42 countries. Each listing includes the history, description and analysis of the brand.

Manual on Treatment of Private Water Supplies   **£7.95**
Department of the Environment, The Welsh Office, The Scottish Office & The Drinking Water Inspectorate, (1993) 65pp.
A clearly written and illustrated manual on obtaining and treating a private water supply. Includes water quality parameters and a comprehensive glossary.

Oxfam Emergency Water Supply Manual   **£1.95**
Oxfam (1988) 8pp.
Information on the purpose and use of Oxfam's kit, which is an essential part of Oxfam's Water Supply Scheme for emergencies and long-term use.

Oxfam Emergency Water Supply Pack   **£19.95**
Oxfam (1992)
A set of manuals to be used with Oxfam's emergency water supply equipment.

Oxfam Well Digging Pack   **£19.95**
Oxfam (1992)
A set of manuals from Oxfam on various aspects of well digging.

The Poisoned Well   **£27.00**
Defence Fund (1989) 400pp.
A critical onslaught on the polluters of American waters.

River Water Quality	**£3.95**
Calow, FSC (1990) 44pp.

The Social and Environmental Effects of Large Dams, Vols. 1-3 £75.00ea
Goldsmith & Hildeyard (eds.), WEC (1984)

Surveillance of Drinking Water Quality in Rural Areas £10.99
Lloyd & Helmer, Longman (1991) 171pp.
Practical guide to improving the service from small water supplies. Suitable for engineers, project managers, sanitary inspectors, environmental health officers and water quality control scientists.

Troubled Water £18.00
Kinnersley, Shipman (1988) 240pp.
The UK experience of rivers, politics and pollution.

Water: The Book £35.00
Barty-King, Quiller (1992) 250pp.
A thoroughly illustrated history of water supply and wastewater in the UK.

Periodicals

Institution of Water Officers
Heriot House, 12 Summerhill Terrace, Newcastle-upon-Tyne NE4 6EB.
Tel. 0191 230 5150 Fax. 0191 230 2880.
Technical feature articles, institution news and reports and articles of a general interest for senior management and engineers within the water and waste industries.

Journal of Water Supply Research & Technology - Aqua
1 Queen Anne's Gate, London SW1H 9BT.
Tel. 0171 957 4567 Fax. 0171 222 7243.
Technical journal of the International Water Supply Association.

Oasis - The WaterAid Journal
1 Queen Anne's Gate, London SW1H 9BT.
Tel. 0171 233 4800 Fax. 0171 233 3161.
News of the WaterAid funded projects around the world.

Water & Environment International
Queensway House, 2 Queensway, Redhill, Surrey RH1 1QS.
Tel. 01737 768611 Fax. 01737 760564.
Covers clean and dirty water treatment,

desalination and irrigation. Also covers allied environmental issues.

Water Bulletin
1 Queen Anne's Gate, London SW1H 9BT.
Tel. 0171 957 4511 Fax. 0171 957 4551.
British water industry news.

Water Services
Queensway House, 2 Queensway, Redhill, Surrey RH1 1QS.
Tel. 01737 768611 Fax. 01737 760564.
Journal covering all aspects of water, both clean and dirty.

Water Supply
1 Queen Anne's Gate, London SW1H 9BT.
Tel. 0171 957 4567 Fax. 0171 222 7243.
Publication of the International Water Supply Association.

Wet News
Turret House, 171 High Street, Rickmansworth,Herts. WD3 1SN.
Tel. 01923 777000 Fax. 01923 771297.
Newspaper for the water and effluent treatment industries.

World Water & Environmental Engineering
Faversham House, 232a Addington Road, Selsdon, South Croydon CR2 8LE.
Tel. 0181 651 7100 Fax. 0181 651 7117.
Journal covering all aspects of the water industry, from developing nations to industrialised areas.

WWT Water & Waste Treatment
Faversham House, 232a Addington Road, Selsdon, South Croydon CR2 8LE.
Tel. 0181 651 7100 Fax. 0181 651 7117.
Magazine covering all aspects of the water industry from potable water to the treatment of effluent.

Index

N E W FUTURES

A series from CAT Publications

The following books are in this series. It is intended to form a comprehensive guide to environmental living, and we recommend obtaining the whole set. Several titles are yet to be published - the anticipated dates are in brackets.

General

Eternal Energy in the Real World Horne, B and Tomalin, E, (January 1997) NF5, 128pp, £6.95

Careers and Courses in Sustainable Technologies Shepherd, A (1995), NF7, 96pp, £5.95

General Technology

Off the Grid: Managing Independent Renewable Electricity Systems Allen, P and Todd, R, (1995) NF6, 60pp, £5.50

Power Plants A Guide to Biofuels Horne, B (1996) NF16, 64pp, £5.50

Wind Power

Where the Wind Blows An Introduction to Wind Power Horne, B, (1994), NF9, 28pp, £3.50

It's a Breeze - A Guide to Choosing Windpower Piggott, H (1995), NF13, 36pp, £4.50

Windpower Workshop, Piggott, H (November 1996), NF14, 160pp, £6.95

Water Power

Going with the Flow: Small Scale Water Power Langley. B and Ramsey, R (October 1996), NF15, 120pp, £7.95

Solar Power

Tapping the Sun: A Solar Water Heating Guide Horne, B (1994), NF1,

16pp, £2.50

Solar Water Heating: A DIY Guide Trimby, P (1994), NF10, 32pp, £3.95

Wired Up to the Sun: A Guide to the Photovoltaic Revolution, Allen,P (1994), NF4, 32pp, £3.95

Energy Conservation

Save Energy Save Money: A Guide to Energy Conservation in the Home, Jackson ,F (1995), NF2, 40pp, £4.50

Environmental Building

Out of the Woods: Ecological Designs for Timber Frame Self Build Borer, P and Harris, C (1994), NF11, 124pp, £12.50

Home and Dry: Ecological Building Design and Materials Borer, P and Harris ,C, (March 1997) NF18 192pp, £8.95

Transport

Getting There: Navigating the Transport Maze Kelly, R (March 1997), NF21, 128pp, £7.95

The Food Cycle

Safe to Drink ? The Quality of Your Water Stauffer, J (1996), NF8, 160pp, £7.95

Sewage Solutions: Answering the Call of Nature Grant, N, Moodie, M and Weedon, C (1996), NF12, 160pp, £8.95

Fertile Waste: Managing Your Domestic Sewage, Harper, P (1994) NF3, 32pp, £3.95

THE CENTRE FOR ALTERNATIVE TECHNOLOGY

... believes in empowering people with practical, positive ways to improve their environment.

You can -

- visit our 10 acre centre where interactive displays demonstrate wind, solar, water and bio-power, sewage treatment, organic gardening, energy conservation, self build and environmental building;

- attend any number of our many residential courses;

- experience 'green living' first hand, as a group, in our purpose built Eco-cabins;

- come as part of a group or school visit, which, where arranged, can include an introductory lecture and guided tour;

- 'buy green by mail' with our extensive mail order service including CAT's own publications;

- contact our Information Department for any queries you may have;

- commission our team of highly experienced consultants - no job too big or small.

Help make a better future. Call us, visit us, write to us, use us!

**Machnylleth, Powys
SY20 9AZ, UK
Tel. 01654 702400**

**Fax. 01654 702782
Email: cat@gn.apc.org
http://www.foe.co.uk/CAT**